Termites
on the Ark

Creative Ideas for Teaching Children

*In memory of my mother,
my first Bible teacher*

Termites
on the Ark

Creative Ideas for Teaching Children

by Pat H. Fulbright

Illustrated by Dana Harrigan

SMYTH&HELWYS
PUBLISHING, INCORPORATED ● MACON, GEORGIA

ISBN 1-57312-171-1

Termites on the Ark
Creative Ideas for Teaching Children

Pat H. Fulbright

Illustrated by Dana Harrigan

The paper used in this publication meets the minimum
requirements of American National Standard for Information Sciences—
Permanence of Paper for Printed Library Materials, ANSI Z39.48-4.

Library of Congress Cataloging-in-Publication Data

Fulbright, Pat H., 1934–
     Termites on the ark: creative ideas for teaching children/
Pat Fulbright.
     Includes index.
     ISBN 1-57312-171-1 (alk. paper)
     1. Christian education of children.
     2. Bible—Study and teaching.
     I. Title.
     BV1475.2.F85   1998
     268'.432—dc21

                                                                            97-50022
                                                                            CIP

Contents

Introduction
FORMULATING: Building Your Own Teaching Rationale

Sara, a fourth-grader, entered the room. She was given a choice of activities. She chose the puppet activity and sat at the table with the other children and her teacher, Mrs. Dawson. They talked about Matthew, one of the writers of the Christmas story, and looked up some of the key verses in their Bibles. Soon the children were called together for large group time during which Mr. Hawkins told the Bible story. At the end he allowed the children to tell about something they thought was relevant to the story. Then Sara went back to her small group.

On the table were small lunch-sized paper bags. "Today we're making puppets," said Mrs. Dawson. She had provided all the necessary supplies and suggested Bible characters to portray: shepherds, angels, Mary, Joseph, and Jesus. Sara and the other children began to work. Sara would not forget the story of the shepherds because she was involved in it. In the next session the group would share the story of Christmas during large group time, using the puppets.

Megan, also a fourth-grader, had quite a different experience. She entered the room. Most of the tables and chairs had been removed, and there was a large open area in the center of the room. On the floor was a "campfire." It was ringed with large "stones" the children had made. The leader had placed flashlights and red cellophane paper inside the stones to simulate a fire. Megan joined a small group and sat on a beanbag chair. The children in her group learned the unit Bible verse and talked about its meaning. Then they gathered for large group time.

The leaders and children sat on the floor around the campfire. At one end of the room sat three shepherds. Each one had a staff lying on the floor and was dressed in a rough-looking costume. At the other end of the room, against the wall, Megan saw a "stable." On the wall behind the stable was a large piece of paper that extended from ceiling to floor. Previously, during small group times, some of the children in the room had drawn pictures on the paper of typical Bible houses with flat roofs, windows, and steps going up the side to the roof. Some of the houses were large, as if to appear close by. Others were small, as if to appear off in the distance. On the floor in front of the stable was a bale of hay. The whole scene looked like a village from biblical times. Bethlehem perhaps?

The lights were turned out in the room. The only light was the light of the "campfire." Mr. Hawkins began to tell the Bible story. He told of the lonely life of a shepherd. The group talked about all the things sheep were used for. "Sheepherding was a dirty, smelly job," said Mr. Hawkins. He paused. One shepherd showed her lunch of raisins, cheese, olives, and bread. Another shepherd showed a double-reed pipe he often used to play as he sang. The third shepherd showed a slingshot she used against wild animals. She also showed how she used her staff to lift sheep out of dangerous places. Mr. Hawkins talked about the visit of one angel to the shepherds and then the appearance of many angels. He said it was dark and scary that night. But the angels had a message: "In David's town, a Savior is born." Megan saw the shepherds quietly stand up and move to the other end of the room to the village scene. They stood in front of the stable while Mr. Hawkins finished telling the story.

When large group time was over, Megan went back to her small group, where she and her friends practiced swaddling a baby using a doll and a large square piece of fabric. They also learned how a newborn Jewish baby was washed and cared for.

When we skim through the Bible, we are immediately struck with the fact that God chose interesting characters to do God's work. They march in a steady line of succession—Adam, Noah, Abraham, and Esther—each taking up where the other left off. They proceed on in steady cadence right through the pages of the New Testament—Peter, Paul, Barnabus, and Dorcas. It is these characters and stories that leaders of children want to present in ways that are informative, challenging, fun, unforgettable, and appealing to the imagination.

This volume is a compilation of challenging and innovative ideas my leaders and I (the department leader) used in the mid-1990s as we attempted to reach children who live in an electronic world. It is intended to be used as a supplement to your present curriculum in any setting in which the Bible is taught. Activities can be adapted according to the needs of your children, the available space and resources, and time allotments. The book is easy to use. Each chapter lists resources and materials, necessary preparation, and class procedures. Supplementary worksheets, songs, and an index are also included.

The contents of this book have been in the making for quite some time. I have "sat at the feet" of some of the best Bible leaders of children: Lillian Moore Rice, Jester Summers, Elsie Rives, Evelyn Vaughn, and Eugene Chamberlain—to name only a few. Their influence on the lives of children will never be forgotten. They knew how to tell stories to make them memorable! My deepest appreciation goes to the following for their help with the actual preparation of the book manuscript: Ridgeway Addison, Eugene Chamberlain, Ramona Conrad, Paul Duke, Mark Lawson, Jo Moore, Tina Newberry, Karen Tye, Jill Ward, and to my ever-patient family.

—Pat H. Fulbright

Chapter 1
IDENTIFYING: Recognizing Factors That Influence Learning*

Laurie is continually reading something that may not relate to the subject at hand. I'm constantly saying, "Laurie, please put that away. We're dealing with something else right now."

Why can't Jeff sit still? He's the most distracting child in this group, like a wiggleworm in hot ashes. He's constantly moving. Why does he demand so much attention? Why can't he be like Chase who sits and listens so attentively and can repeat much of what we say?

Why must Tim always have something in his hands—a string, a rubberband, anything to distract everyone else? During every session something has to be taken away from him.

Kelly talks repeatedly and whispers to the children around her. She is continually speaking out. She's very disruptive. We've talked to her about it, but she doesn't seem to want to change.

Andy refuses to write anything. He won't participate. And yet he's very smart. He can repeat a Bible verse after hearing it one time. He can remember things well without writing them down. I'm afraid the other children in the group will feel they don't have to participate either.

Carrie becomes restless when merely listening to a story. But when pictures or objects are visible that relate to a Bible story, she is an avid listener.

Ray loved the day we made a display of barley and wheat bread. He even volunteered to find out the difference between the two grains and report to the group.

What's going on here? Most likely, each of these children represents a different learning style.

> Laurie is doing what comes naturally. She may be a print-oriented learner. She learns best through reading and writing, and retains easily what she reads.

> Jeff may be a kinesthetic learner. He learns best while moving. He has to move some part of his body while processing information.

> Tim may be a tactile learner. He absorbs information through touching or feeling objects. He needs hands-on experiences.

> Kelly may not be obstinate; she may be an interactive learner. She learns best through verbalization. She seems to thrive on disagreeing, rivalry, and being able to express her opinions critically.

> Andy may be an aural learner. He generally learns best through listening. Verbal presentation of information is important to him.

> Carrie may be a visual learner. She learns best through observation. She likes to see visual stimuli such as bulletin boards, pictures, slides, graphs, tables, and demonstrations.

> Ray may be an olfactory learner. He learns best by associating information with a particular smell or taste.[1]

A learning style is a combination of how we perceive, or become aware, and how we process, or work with the reality after we perceive it. This combination of perceiving and processing forms the uniqueness of our learning style, our most comfortable way to learn.[2] In other words,

1

certain behaviors indicate how we learn from and adapt to our environment. These behaviors are clues to how our minds operate. Thus, a learning style is the outward display of the workings of the mind. It is our way of taking in new information and making sense of it. As we comprehend new information, we digest it and filter it through our own experiences. For example, a group of inner-city school children in Houston, Texas, identified a squirrel in a movie as a rat. Some of us jump right in and try new information; others of us sit back and think about it.

So, why is it important for us as leaders to be aware of learning styles? Typically, we tend to teach according to our own best learning style. And it could be that those students who are the most difficult to control and who take up most of our attention are those whose learning styles don't match the approach to teaching we're using. For instance, if we repeatedly propose pencil and paper activities, then those children who prefer to listen rather than write could fail to harmonize. Behavior and learning problems can result.

Influences on Learning

How do we develop learning styles? There are four primary influences: biology or genetics, personality, life experiences, and circumstances of our present situation. Economic level is a secondary influence. In addition, certain environmental conditions can affect learning: physical space, time of day, stage of physical and emotional development, and perhaps weather and color. Here these elements are addressed in particular reference to children.

BIOLOGY, PERSONALITY, LIFE EXPERIENCES, PRESENT CIRCUMSTANCES

Children may be predisposed to certain approaches to learning. Their general biological makeup, the way their muscles work, and visual or hearing disabilities can influence how they learn. Their personalities also can affect how they approach learning.

Different children develop different personalities even if they are reared in the same family. For example, introverted children avoid interaction with others, whereas extroverted children prefer to work in a group. Life experiences also can influence how children learn.

Where children are born, who their parents are, what part of the country they live in, and the nature of their neighborhoods are all part of who they are. They may be born into a family that teaches the value of working with one's hands, or perhaps into a family in which reading has high priority. They may be suffering from shattered dreams, broken bones, deep emotional scars, or abandoned hearts. Current circumstances also shape learning.

Even though children in schools represent a variety of learning styles, schools tend to focus primarily on visual and oral learning styles. Children may have to manage those styles in order to succeed, even though those are not their preferred styles.

ECONOMIC LEVEL

In addition to genetic makeup, personality, life experiences, and present circumstances, economic level also can affect learning. Quite often, children from low-income levels are born to teenage mothers. Pregnant teenagers are more likely to have babies with a low birth weight, a condition often associated with mental handicaps such as learning disabilities. Learning-disabled children cannot handle large projects and detailed instructions.

Some children from low economic levels may not have the opportunity to meet many people or to travel. They may lack social skills. Their parents may not converse with each other about important events. There may be little structure in their homes, and meals and bedtimes may not be at fixed times. In many cases, these may be homes where there are few books or little music to stimulate the minds. Families may rent rather than own their homes. Therefore, they may not have pride in their homes and yards, and, consequently, no respect for equipment elsewhere. They may never expect to have homes of their own, or jobs, or support. There are no boundaries or consistency in the homes and, therefore, little security.

Children from low-income levels who have been shifted from place to place and family to family may feel they have no control over their own lives. They may have attachment disorders and, as a result, may never bond with anyone again. These children also are likely to have problems with low self-esteem because our society does not value the poor. Also, poor parents have to focus on survival, which does not leave much time to provide a nurturing environment. They lack encouragement, success, and opportunities for making choices.

SPACE, TIME OF DAY, DEVELOPMENT

Some children need a cool environment in order to concentrate; others prefer to feel warm. Some children may get drowsy in an overly-warm room; others may find it hard to concentrate if the room is very cold. Likewise, children respond differently to the amount of light in the room. Some think better in areas that are dimly lit, while others require bright illumination. Some respond to excessive light by becoming hyper-active; others become drowsy in dim light.

Atmosphere and noise level also can affect children. Some thrive in an informal atmosphere such as sitting on carpet, pillows, or beanbag chairs. Others cannot handle the variety of stimulation, so they learn better in a structured arrangement of desks or tables. Some children learn perfectly well in noisy surroundings; others

must learn in quiet, peaceful places. Some leaders don't want to teach in noisy surroundings. Perhaps they are themselves students who learn best in a quiet atmosphere.

Time of day also can affect concentration and retention. Some students work better early before the day takes its toll on their energy. For them, the time after lunch might be an unproductive time of day. Therefore, outdoor activities and/or more interactive learning may be needed for the latter part of the day.

Finally, because mental age and chronological age may not correlate, all children need tasks they can achieve. Success in achievement will lead to happiness and the desire to succeed again. Repeated failure may cause difficulty later in life with other tasks. Focusing on one simple lesson during a session may be better than presenting too many facts children cannot grasp. Also, some students work best in an atmosphere in which the emotional tone is low-key and interpersonal conflicts are softened.

Learning Styles

In addition to biological, social, economic, and environmental factors that influence learning, there are varieties of ways to learn. All children have preferred methods for learning, methods that may not prove to be as useful to others. Put simply, leaders cannot teach a lesson to an entire class and expect everyone to understand it in the same way. When taught in ways that complement their own learning preferences, children become motivated and, therefore, learn more.

Leaders often say, "How can they be learning when they aren't listening?" Some children require absolute silence when they are concentrating; others block out background noises. Some may even require sound when they are seeking to learn, for example, adolescents who must have music in the background in order to study.

It could be that the most well-behaved, well-liked, and seemingly most intelligent students have managed to find their niche—by matching their learning style with the style that is being taught. Yet, all children have a preferred learning style, whether visual, auditory, tactile, or kinesthetic.

VISUAL LEARNERS

Some learners need to see objects—a boat, a fishnet, sandals—when hearing a story. These visual learners remember what they see, for instance, the events of a movie or TV show. They enjoy library and museum visits. They like books, puzzles, and pictures. They need colors, shapes, images, maps, and drawings. Visual learners won't be helped much by lectures. These children need structured, step-by-step processes. They need to see on paper what they have done and the ongoing results of it. These children may do well with the Searching Stop (see p. 9).

AUDITORY LEARNERS

Sound is important to auditory learners. They will sing to you theme songs and jingles. They love storytelling and music. They need lots of time to talk. They need vibrations, rhythms, oral directions, tape recordings, and sound effects. These children may do well in the Music Stop (see p. 10).

TACTILE LARNERS

Tactile learners need opportunities to touch things, such as flowers, furry animals, rocks, and trees. Usually, they are creative and self-motivated, and thus do well with choice-making activities. These children may do well with the Rest Stop (see p. 10).

KINESTHETIC LEARNERS

Some children need body movements—acting, dancing, marching, and gesturing. These may be your drama buffs. They may not have a long attention span for programmed materials, and sometimes may refuse to participate in this type of learning altogether. But they learn even when they appear not to be listening. Kinesthetic learners may not do well with the Rest Stop unless some of their tasks are to go and find/do something in another location.

Children learn new information through sight, sound, touch, or experience. This does not mean that children who prefer one style cannot learn through another style. It does mean that children generally understand lessons better and more easily through their own preferred style.

Damaged Learners

> Heyward's father is an alcoholic who doesn't work and beats his children as a means of discipline. There are 11 children in the family. The oldest is in drug rehabilitation; the youngest is 2. The family is on public assistance. Heyward has moved a lot. He is continually berated and subsequently bullies other children. His self-esteem is low. How can Heyward ever see God as being forgiving?

> Phylis is a victim of incest. She has hearing problems. She lives with her mother, stepfather, and 5 brothers. The children are often left to care for themselves. Phylis does not have good personal hygiene. How can she "trust Jesus" when she can't trust those closest to her?

> Both of Angie's parents are chemically dependent. Angie often has to be the parent to her 4 brothers and sisters. She has lost her childhood. She lives with emotional and physical abuse. How can Angie believe in an unchanging God when she lives with the unpredictable and inconsistent behavior of her addicted parents?

> Bradley lives with his grandmother. He has 3 younger sisters and 3 younger brothers. His mother left the family. His opinions are never

valued. Why should he talk to a God he can't see when those people he can see aren't interested in listening to him?

> Wesley is age 11. He has 1 older brother and 3 younger brothers. He lives with his mother and stepfather, who often leave the children alone to fend for themselves. Wesley has lived in 8 houses and attended 5 different schools. How can Wesley believe that God will take care of him when his family doesn't take care of him?

> Francine's mother is an alcoholic. However, the family fares very well financially. Francine is desperate to please, hoping to avoid her mother's wrath. What will be Francine's reaction to the news that she is a sinner? Will it reinforce what she's felt all along: "I'm no good, I can't do anything right. I'm worthless?" Will she make a faith commitment much too soon in a desperate attempt to please and to wipe away the "sinner" label?

> Bo is almost 13. He's the oldest child among 5. Some children make fun of Bo's speech patterns. He is often overlooked because he acts differently, talks differently, and was not previously in a particular group of friends. How can Bo relate to the news that Jesus loves everyone?

> Mark has 5 siblings. His older brothers are leaders in a neighborhood gang. He has moved 5 times and has been in many schools. His father is in prison. In a world in which bad guys often have flashy cars and beautiful clothes, will Mark see the rewards of being good? How can he see God as a kind and dependable "father" who is always there when needed, when his own father is never there for him?

> Catherine is the only child of a wealthy family. Her father is kind and generous but hardly ever at home. Her mother provides very little discipline and often makes—and breaks—promises. Catherine is a loner. She feels that no one delights in her. Will Catherine "act out" because

her emotional needs aren't being met? How can she believe that God thinks of her as important?

Some children live stressful lives. They may be needy, emotionally damaged, angry, or neglected. These are "damaged learners," or students who are physically normal but damaged in self-esteem, intellect, and social give-and-take. They reject learning. They daydream but pretend to absorb everything taught.[3] In order to concentrate on learning, children need freedom from emotional disturbances at home, school, and church.

To increase their motivation level, damaged learners may require short assignments, much supervision, simple objectives, and lots of praise and feedback while they are working to reinforce their learning. They may need color, for their surroundings are often drab. They may need field trips, for they may not have traveled far from their schools. Others may need to learn how to work with others. Team-building experiences can help them to become more tolerant of others. Perhaps some learners have been dominated by other people and have been allowed to make few choices. These children may need constant guidance from and accountability to an adult. However, all damaged learners have one primary need: unconditional love.

Conclusion

As leaders we need to be willing to expand our teaching styles in order to cater to the learning styles of all our students, always taking into consideration the biological, social, economic, and psychological factors that influence each child's learning. When the learning style of a child and the teaching style of a leader are matched, significant results appear. The best approach is to gradually expand the range of teaching styles in order to accommodate more and more children. Include cassette tapes to appeal to the auditory learner. Include the use of films or videos to reinforce the learning of visually-oriented

IDENTIFYING

children. Create more discussion in small groups, and interactive learners will likely join in with greater enthusiasm.

To achieve maximum learning, always teach in a way that encourages the strengths of every child in the room, and teach in ways that invite the children to try new learning styles—which may open them up to learnings that would not be possible with their usual style. Therefore, develop a repertoire of styles. After all, the real test of children's learning lies in their ability to apply it to life.

Notes

[1]From Waynne James and Michael Galbraith, in "Perceptual Learning Styles: Implications and Techniques for the Practitioner," in *Lifelong Learning* (January 1985): 20-23.

[2]Adapted from David A. Kolb, Irwin M. Rubin, and James M. McIntyre, *Organizational Psychology: An Experiential Approach*, 3d ed. (Upper Saddle River NJ: Simon and Schuster, 1979).

[3]Adapted from Barb and Louis Fischer, "Styles in Teaching and Learning," in *Educational Leadership* (January 1979): 245-54. Reprinted by permission of the Association for Supervision and Curriculum Development. Copyright ©1985 by ASCD. All rights reserved.

*The contents of this chapter are based on an interview with Dr. Karen Tye, St. Louis MO, 13 September 1995.

Chapter 2
PREPARING: Providing an Exciting Learning Environment

Rationale

The setting, or environment, in which children learn is of great significance. Environment is not just the room setting but the warmth and welcome felt there. It is the mood and caring concern of the leaders. Environment influences behavior. A well-planned room gives children self-esteem. It makes them think, "I'm important; I'm welcome; Someone expected me to come." Psychologists agree that a relaxed, informal atmosphere leads to the most learning. Fun, combined with firm discipline, signals learning. Every inch of the room, including the wall, the floor, even the ceiling and the corners, has a learning potential.

The learning environment does not have to be a perfect setting or furnished with expensive equipment. The size of teaching rooms will vary from church to church and building to building. Some children meet in a choir loft or an open area in the hall or a corner of a church sanctuary. You may choose to teach in the more traditional way with tables and chairs in the room. You may wish to take a new approach to the room setting and remove existing tables and chairs. Either the old or the new setting can be used with most any curriculum resource, with different units of study, and in large and small group times.

In this chapter you will find a list of resources and necessary preparations for the large and small group areas and also suggestions for making numerous props to ensure more effective teaching and learning.

Large Group

PREPARING

RESOURCES
appliance box (30"x30"x40")
blankets for bedrolls
blue painted paper (for body of water)
cardboard
carpet
cassette tape of Israeli folk songs
chalk
chalk/markerboard
clothespins (for attaching items to rope)
clothes rack (for displays, costumes, charts, etc.)
colored construction paper
dishwashing detergent
duct tape
felt tip pens
flashlight
freezer tape loops (for hanging pictures)
game box (with activities and teaching aids)
garbage can (30 gallon)
(use for well/wrap with stone-painted paper)
glue
green blanket (hillside)
jellybeans
maps
masking tape
modeling clay or homemade playdough
(Mix 1 cup flour and 1 cup salt. Add enough water to make mixture pliable. Add 1 TBS oil.)
newspaper (several thicknesses for window covers)
paint
paper
paper towels
pencils
pushpins
rope (for hanging pictures, time lines)
scissors
sink
sponges
staples
stepladder (4')
table paper
teaching pictures
wall hooks (to connect rope)
window shades

*Some large group resources are used in study stops.

PREPARATION
> Discard materials from past units of study.

> Leave empty wall space for displays.

> Set up a small desk in the hall for keeping records.

> Plan a color scheme for the room.

> Remove existing tables and chairs. Then bring into the room a couple of folding tables and several child-sized chairs. Or start with a sparsely furnished room by stacking tables and chairs to gain more space.

> Assemble alternate seating for the children (see p. 9). Borrow seating supplies from other areas in the room when needed. Provide large chairs for the leaders, although often they will sit on the floor.

> Make plenty of open space in the center of the room.

> Position small group activities anywhere in the room where space allows. If you use study stops, you may wish to place the groups between the stops.

> Paint metal and plastic items bright colors.

> Make lapboards of 12"x15" pieces of cardboard covered with table paper. Place them in the room where the children can retrieve them whenever needed. (These will replace the need for tables.)

> Reinforce the inside seams of an appliance box with duct tape. Turn the box upside down. Cut a door just large enough for a child to enter. Paint it a bright color. Place a flashlight inside for quiet reading time. When used for reading,

display a sign that reads, "Only 1 child at a time, please." The box can be left in the room at all times and used for the cave/stable in the Christmas story, a tomb, a prison, etc. Make a house by attaching steps made from cardboard to the sides of the box. If you use it for a house, ask the children to name what might be inside, for example, bedrolls stored in a chest, cooking utensils hanging on a wall, a cookfire, a waterjar, rugs.

*Think portable rather than stationary furnishings and equipment. Make their uses as versatile as possible. For example, the 4' stepladder has many uses: for seating Jesus to teach the Sermon on the Mount, for sending Moses to the top of Mt. Sinai, for stationing a guard on the city wall, for positioning Zacchaeus in a tree, for making a stairway to heaven for Jacob, for making a fun seat for children. Also, at various times you may wish to transform the room into . . .

- a well in Midian
- a field outside Bethlehem
- the Sinai Desert
- a Roman prison
- a caravan route
- a New Testament house
- the garden of Eden
- a modern-day home
- a stable
- an Israelite village
- a synagogue
- an upper room
- a temple
- the garden of Gethsemane
- Solomon's Porch
- the pool of Siloam
- a threshing floor
- the marketplace
- the wilderness of Judea

*If you cannot afford some of the suggested equipment and supplies, advertise in the church/school newspaper or bulletin for donations. Visit garage sales and thrift stores.

PROCEDURE
Play background music of Israeli folk songs.

For large group time, children will sit in their small groups but turn to face the large group leader for the Bible story.

Expand your teaching area. Examples: Go outside and sit on bedsheets on the grass; sit on steps or stairs; use chalk to make a sidewalk or parking lot map; mark trees to designate the location of cities and countries to get an idea of distances; go to a barn for the Christmas story or to a hill for the crufixion story.

Small Group Time

Small Group Time

Small Groups

• Use these seating items interchangeably: 4-gallon metal bucket turned upside down, large colorful pillows, small rugs, stool, 4' stepladder, tires, beanbag chairs, hassock, 30-gallon garbage can turned upside down with a small rug on the top, a few child-sized chairs, several old tires. You may want to add a claw-foot bathtub with pillows for reading.

• As children arrive, help them choose which small group to join (6-7 maximum per group). Options: Hand out colored jellybeans that coordinate with a bowl of jellybeans at each leader's area; allow each child to choose a 2″ square of colored construction paper that matches the color of each small group area.

Study Stops

SEARCHING STOP (see Chap. 10)

RESOURCES
appliance box
atlas
Bible dictionary
Bibles (several translations)
bookcase or stacked painted wooden or cardboard boxes
cassette player
commentary (1 volume)
concordance
duct tape
electrical outlet
flashlight
folding table
index cards (4″x6″)
ironing board
maps
newspaper and magazine clippings
paper
pencils
picture books of Bible lands
pictures from old curriculum
sign: "Searching Stop"
sign for appliance box
stepladder (2')
vinyl picnic tablecloth

PREPARATION

> Make signs for study stops.

> Display the sign: "Searching Stop."

> Set up a folding table. Cover with a colorful vinyl picnic tablecloth.

> Set up an ironing board to use as a writing stand or for making things with the hands.

> Place on a table these materials: paper (lined for younger children), pencils, 4"x6" index cards, a bookcase, informative articles and pictures from old curriculum materials, large teaching pictures, several Bible translations, a tape player, a 1-volume commentary, a Bible dictionary, a concordance, an atlas, maps, picture books of Bible lands, and a box of current newspaper and magazine clippings.

PROCEDURE

Children will assemble an alphabetized resource notebook, regularly adding helpful materials based on their reading level.

Children will do research both for personal use and for sharing in large group time.

REST STOP (see Chap. 13)

RESOURCES
accordian-fold pattern cutting board or a cardboard box
box cutter
bulletin board
felt tip pens
floor lamp
lapboards
paper
pencils
pillow
rug
sign: "Rest Stop"
supplies for suggested activities
tire

PREPARATION

> Make and display sign.

> Using a box at least 27" tall, cut out 1 side, the bottom, and the top, so that the 2 remaining sides fan out to make it a stand-up. Cover the box with paper. Display the instructions for the activities. Or, display instructions on an accordian-fold pattern cutting board or on an existing bulletin board.

> On the floor place a rug, pillow, and an old tire for seating. A floor lamp is a nice addition.

> Supply pencils, felt tip pens, and paper.

> Furnish any supplies for activities suggested for each unit.

> Place supplies on the floor.

> Change the contents for every unit of study.

PROCEDURE

Provide 5-6 activities for individual use by early arrivers, visitors, problem children, or children who finish another activity early.

MUSIC STOP (see Chap. 14)

RESOURCES
autoharp
cassette player
electrical outlet
folding table
hymnals
metal garbage can or wastebasket
musical instruments
pillow
recorded songs
sign: "Music Stop"
stool

PREPARATION

> Make and display sign.

> Provide seating: a stool, an upside-down wastebasket, and a large pillow.

> Set up a folding table.

> On the table place a tape player, recorded songs, hymnals, and an autoharp and other musical instruments.

> If you have a piano, donate it to another group and use music on a cassette tape, or give it double duty. If the room is average in size, let the back of the piano face another area. Cover it with cardboard or fabric. Use it to display placards, pictures, etc.

PROCEDURE

Provide activities for small group participation or individual research.

THINK STOP (see Chap. 5)

RESOURCES
beanbag chair
chairs (child-size)
pillows
sign: "Think Stop"
tire

PREPARATION

> Locate in a quiet area near the large group room. (One leader arranged this stop in an open space beside the steps going up to the sanctuary. The steps could also be used as a place to sit.)

> Make and display sign.

> Include a beanbag chair, large pillows, an old tire, and a few small chairs.

PROCEDURE

Provide a quiet place for children (individuals or groups) to ponder, examine their feelings, and do creative writing. Provide needed supplies.

Making Props

RESOURCES
aluminum foil
cardboard boxes
cleaner for paintbrushes
cord or rope
dowel sticks
elastic
felt tip pens
foil (gold and silver)
freezer wrap or shelf paper
gift ribbon
glasses (inexpensive plastic and/or glass)
glue
illustrations of the items you plan to make
long sticks
long tables covered with paper
masking tape
metal garbage can lid
modeling clay or homemade playdough
narrow elastic
newspaper
paint stirrers
paintbrushes (different sizes)
paints (acrylic, enamel, spray, tempera)
paper grocery bags (small/large)
paper towels
pencils
pizza
plastic spray
posterboard (i.e., white and gold or yellow)
rags
ribbon
scissors
sealer/primer
sewing machine
staples
table paper
vinyl material or imitation leather

PREPARATION

> At the beginning of a new year with your children, invite them and their leaders to a "Pizza, Props, and Paint Party" to be held in someone's backyard on a Saturday.

> Purchase supplies and pizza and/or ask for donations.

PREPARING

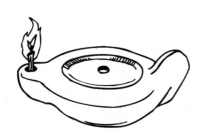

Animal backdrops

Oil lamp

Egyptian fan

PROCEDURE

Allow children to paint room furnishings such as ladders, stools, and tire seats. (Paint does not adhere well to rubber, so, when painting the tires, apply several coats of sealer/primer first and then the colored paint.)

Allow children to make props. (Note: Some props can be bought more easily than made, for example, a bow and arrow, a cluster of artificial grapes, and baskets.) Listed below in alphabetical order are some useful props and suggestions for making them.

• *Animal backdrops*: On separate sheets of table paper paint a backdrop of the heads and necks of several types of animals.

• *Bowls, cups, oil lamps*: Use self-hardening clay or a salt-and-flour mixture. Roll clay into a ball. Push your thumb into the center. Continue shaping the ball. Dry at room temperature or bake. Paint with tempera or acrylic paint. Dry. Spray with plastic spray.

• *Coins*: On posterboard draw outlines around quarters, nickels, and dimes. Cut out outlines. Cover with gold and silver foil. Place inside money bags.

• *Egyptian fan*: Cut a piece of cardboard into the shape of a fan. Color with felt tip pens or colored pencils. Attach to a long stick.

• *Goblets*: Buy inexpensive glass or plastic goblets. Spray paint gold or silver.

• *Oven*: Make from a flat, Frisbee-shaped object. For fuel, use dried brush or branches.

• *Prison chains*: Make a chain of loops from posterboard or heavy paper. Make cuffs on either side of the chain for wrists and ankles to fit into. Spray paint black.

• *Scrolls*: Use long pieces of shelf paper or freezer wrap. Write Scripture passages or other messages on the paper. Using tape, attach the paper to 1″-thick dowel sticks. Roll the sticks towards each other, with the copied passages on the inside. Tie with solid-colored gift ribbon.

• *Seed bags*: Make a large and a small bag from imitation leather. (The large bag will fit on the back of a donkey, and the small one under the farmer's arm.)

• *Sheaves of grain*: Draw and cut outlines from cardboard boxes. Spray paint yellow. Draw details in brown. Draw a tie around the center.

• *Shield*: Cut large round or square pieces out of a cardboard box. Cover with aluminum foil. On the back attach elastic (for the child's arm). Or, attach a round piece of posterboard to the back of a metal garbage can lid, making it a solid surface. (The child will use the handle on the front side to hold the shield.) Spray paint silver.

• *Shophar*: Using white posterboard, cut 2 shapes of a ram's horn 18″ long. Fill with crushed newspaper to make a rounded shape. Tape the 2 sides together. Spray paint white.

• *Sickle*: Cut a flat outline from cardboard. Spray paint the blade silver and the handle tan or brown.

• *Slingshot*: Use braided cord or leather to make a cup 2″ wide and 5″ long to hold a stone. Attach 2 long pieces of cord or leather to the sides.

• *Spear*: Attach a sharp point made from posterboard to the end of a long stick. Spray paint silver.

• *Staff*: Attach a crook made of posterboard or cardboard to the end of a long stick. Spray paint tan or brown.

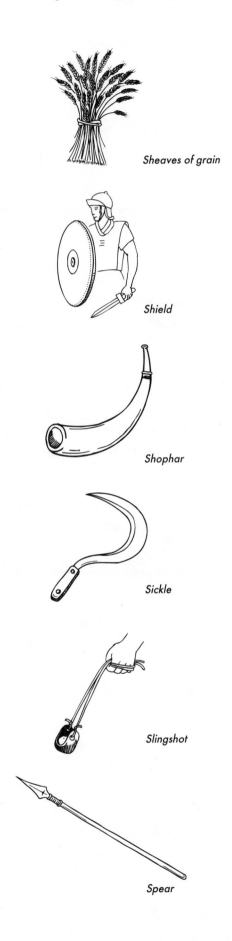

Sheaves of grain

Shield

Shophar

Sickle

Slingshot

Spear

- *Stones*: Crush newspaper into different sized balls. Cover with pieces of table paper. Tape with masking tape. Spray paint gray.

- *Stone covering*: Paint a long piece of table paper gray and white. Wrap painted paper around a 30-gallon garbage can turned right side up to resemble a well. Place painted paper on the floor or wall to resemble a jail or prison.

- *Sword*: Cut out shape from cardboard boxes. Spray paint silver.

- *Temple Vessels*: Stuff large paper grocery bags with crushed newspaper. Fill ¾ of the way up. Wrinkle and mold the bags at the top. Around the neck, wrap masking tape or a strip of paper sack 1″ wide. Spray paint gold or silver.

- *Waterbag*: Cut imitation leather (vinyl) into the shape of a goat. Sew up the holes where the legs and tail would have been. Leave the neck area open to form the mouth of the bottle.

- *Water jars*: Stuff large paper grocery bags with crushed newspaper. Fill ¾ of the way up. Wrinkle and mold the bags at the top. Around the neck, wrap masking tape or a strip of paper sack 1″ wide. Attach a handle. Spray paint tan or brown.

- *Winnowing fork*: Cut 2 flat outlines of a large fork. Staple together. Leave an opening at the bottom. Insert a broomstick. Spray paint tan.

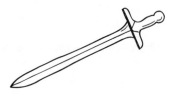

Sword

Waterbag

Water jar

Winnowing fork

Chapter 3
PERCEIVING: Learning about Eastern Customs

Rationale

The Bible had its origin in the East, yet most of us read into the Bible Western manners and customs. Many Scriptures that are hard for us to understand are easily explained by a knowledge of manners and customs of biblical lands.

In the seventh century, many Arabs broke away from Arabia and invaded the Near East. They brought with them habits inherited from countless generations. Since then they have become the preservers of the manners and customs of Bible times. For centuries these customs have been largely unchanged with some exceptions, most having to do with religious observances. We are indebted to the Arabs for our understanding of Jewish customs. The findings of archaeologists also provide essential knowledge.[1]

Learning about Eastern culture and customs can help children better understand the biblical stories. This chapter focuses on some of these customs and their relationship to our present religious practices.

The Planting and Harvesting of Grain

RESOURCES
barley
barley bread
colander or piece of wire
pictures of modern-day farm machinery
picture of a threshing floor
"sheaves of grain"
"sickle"
wheat
wheat bread
"winnowing fork"

PREPARATION
> Purchase dry barley and wheat and barley and wheat bread at a health food store.

> Make sheaves of grain (see p. 13), a sickle (see p. 13), and a winnowing fork (see p. 14).

PROCEDURE
Make Searching Stop assignments. Ask several children to find information about planting and harvesting grain. Ask a child to find a picture of a threshing floor. Ask for reports to the large group.

Show pictures of modern-day farm machinery. Discuss how valuable farmers are to us. Say, *People of biblical times did not have farm machinery. Their work had to be done by hand. All of us know what planting is. When planting, farmers of biblical times carried seed to their fields in large sacks on the backs of donkeys and then scattered the seed over the ground. Then someone went behind the farmers with ploughs, or instruments used for breaking up the ground and then covering the seed with dirt. Farmers also left narrow paths without seed for travelers to walk on.*

Ask, *Do you know what harvesting is?* Ask a child to define the word based on her findings in the Searching Stop. Explain, *The farmers grew 2 kinds of grain: wheat and barley. The poor people ate bread made from barley, and the prosperous people ate bread made from wheat.*

The children may need an explanation of planting and harvesting grain for the stories of Ruth, Gideon's call, or Jesus' parables. Present the following information at appropriate sessions to help children understand the harvesting of grain.

The barley harvest came about the time of the Feast of the Passover in the spring. All the people of a village went to the fields to help farmers harvest their crops. Men and women sang harvest songs. Little children played together while their parents worked. Men used sickles to cut the grain. They held the stalks of barley in their left hands and cut them with their right hands. Ask a child to pantomime the cutting of the barley. *Then the women gathered the stalks and tied them into bundles, or sheaves, bound with straw.* See Genesis 37:5-8. Point out the sheaves of grain. *The boys then loaded the sheaves of grain onto the backs of donkeys or camels and took them to the threshing floor.*

An interesting custom allowed women to glean, or gather, grain after the harvesters finished. You'll remember that Ruth did this. See Ruth 2:2, 3. *Many poor women without husbands came to glean. Also, some grain was always purposely left in the corners of the fields when it was harvested. This was for the poor, beggars, and hungry travelers who passed by. People often ate the grain raw right out of the field.* See Luke 6:1.

After being bound into sheaves, the grain was taken to the threshing floor. This floor was a circular space. The dirt had been smoothed and beaten very hard. The grain was placed on the floor about 2' deep, and oxen walked over

it. By this method, the grain was rubbed from the heads of wheat or barley. Being heavier, the grain sank through the straw. The straw was crushed and later used as food for animals or to make bricks.

Sometimes farmers used "sledges" to separate grain from straw. Sledges had a board with pieces of stone or iron set into the bottom surface. Oxen pulled sledges across the grain. Small amounts of grain could also be beaten against the ground by hand to free the grain. See Ruth 2:17. Ask a child to show the picture of the threshing floor.

Then it was time to separate straw and chaff from the good grain. Broad shovels or large wooden winnowing forks, also called "fans," were used. Winnowers used the large forks or shovels to throw heaps of grain into the air. Since the grain was heaviest, it fell to the ground fastest. The wind blew the straw to the side into a mound, and the lighter chaff, or worthless husks of wheat, were blown by the wind even further away and were later burned. See Ruth 3:2, Psalm 1:4, and Matthew 3:12. Ask a child to illustrate winnowing, using a shovel or winnowing fork.

Then women sifted the grain to make sure all the straw and chaff were out. They put the grain into sieves, containers having small holes in the bottom. If any chaff was left, the women blew it away with their breath. They also removed any mud or stones from the grain. Ask two children to demonstrate this, using a small colander or piece of wire as a strainer.

Then the finished grain was stored in large jars underneath the ground where it was kept secret by covering the opening. Since bread was the main food of the people of Israel, they had to protect the grain that was used for making it. The grain was stored in "storehouses," also known as "garners" or "barns."

The storage jars for the grain may have looked similar to the water jars shown on p. 14.

Bread was important to the people. The people believed it was a blessing from God. The grain was ground by the women with a millstone in order to make flour, which was then used to make bread. See p. 107. *Grain was sold to people at the marketplace.* See p. 82. Show the dry barley and wheat to the children. Break small pieces of barley bread and wheat bread for the children to taste. *Isn't it great to know that, in our time, we can just buy a loaf of bread?*

Belshazzar's Feast

RESOURCES
artificial grapes
baskets
costumes (elegant and simple)
"crown"
"gold chain"
"gold goblets"
gold spray paint
"handwriting on the wall"
invitations
Oriental rug (small)
"pendant"
pillows
posterboard
purple fabric
seedless grapes
table
tambourine
taped music (Israeli folk songs)
"temple vessels"
"throne"
yellow construction paper

PREPARATION
> A week before the session, send out invitations containing information similar to the following:

You're Invited to a Party
Date: Sunday, September 25
Time: 9:00 A.M.
Place: First Baptist Church, Room 104
Given by: King Belshazzar
Please come and be prepared for anything!

> Make a gold chain: Cut loops from yellow construction paper. Glue together. Spray paint gold.

> Make a pendant: Cover an oval-shaped piece of posterboard 3″ long. Attach it at the bottom of the chain to rest on a child's chest. Spray paint gold. Place it just outside the room.

> Read about Daniel's character and faith in God (see pp. 66, 67) and about King Nebuchadnezzar's conquest of Jerusalem and his taking away of the captives (see p. 66).

> Move the room's furnishings against the wall.

> Arrange the center of the room like the inside of a king's palace.

> Place a small Oriental rug on the floor.

> Scatter rich-looking fabrics and pillows around the room.

> Place some purple artificial grapes and gold goblets on a table.

> On the floor in front of the table place several gold and silver temple vessels (see p. 14).

> Provide some handwriting on the wall.

17

PROCEDURE

Dress a child as Daniel. Wrap a long piece of fabric around her shoulders. Ask her to wait outside the room. Dress another child as King Belshazzar. Drape purple fabric around his shoulders. Place a crown on his head. Seat him on his throne (a chair). Dress another child as the servant. Drape a much less dignified fabric around her shoulders. Dress two children in servant costumes.

As the party begins, play taped music and a tambourine in the background. Ask the servants to pass around baskets of seedless grapes.

Ask, *How did Daniel get to Babylon, where we find him in today's story?* Tell the story:

King Nebuchadnezzar was pleased with Daniel and his friends when they were healthy, even though they refused to eat the rich food he gave them. Also, this king had disturbing dreams, and Daniel was able to interpret them. When Nebuchadnezzar died, his son Belshazzar took his place. Don't confuse this name with Belteshazzar. That was the new name Daniel was given in Babylon. See Daniel 1:7.

Belshazzar did not fear Daniel's God. He gave a large feast for many people in Babylon. He even had the nerve to use the beautiful vessels his father had captured from the temple in Jerusalem for all his friends to drink from. Point to the vessels. *This was* not *a good party, and probably everyone was drunk.*

It was Daniel's custom to pray to God a lot both day and night. Even his enemies could not stop him from praying. Because of this, Daniel was able to please God while living in a pagan, or sinful, land without doing wrong things himself. Daniel was a missionary. In this story we can especially see how God was able to give Daniel wisdom.

Relate the incident of the handwriting on the wall as found in Daniel 5:1-9. Say, *The king was so frightened that he turned pale, and his knees knocked together.*

Do the following playacting: Ask the servant to bring Daniel in. The king and Daniel pantomime their conversation. Then the servant goes out and gets the gold chain, which the king places over Daniel's head. Make it clear that King Belshazzar also made Daniel the third highest ruler in the kingdom.

Ask, *Does this story remind you of another man in the Bible who refused to disobey God and was made a great ruler because of his great abilities? He, too, could interpret dreams.* Joseph. *Could some of our world leaders learn a lesson from these two men? Are there rewards in obeying God's rules? Can you think of other Bible stories that make this lesson clear?*

Ask, *Suppose in a few years you go to a party. Everyone is drinking alcoholic beverages except you. Some guests may even be drunk. But you feel you don't need to drink those drinks. How will you handle that situation?* Give the children time to answer. They may give suggestions such as: call my parents to come and get me; ask my date to take me home; tell the group courageously that I will drink other things, but not alcohol. *Suppose the problem is cigarettes or some other drug besides alcohol? What will these things do to your body?*

Say, *Daniel was able to obey God in a sinful world because he made up his mind ahead of time what he would say and do. Would that be a good rule for you? People will begin to watch your "customs" and perhaps follow your example. Daniel wasn't just an ordinary man; he was a super hero, one whose example you and I would do well to follow.*

Burial Customs

RESOURCES
Bibles
cardboard or posterboard
costumes (2 simple men's and women's)
large appliance box
large, flat, round "stone"
linen cloth
strips of cloth
table paper

PREPARATION
> Cut cloth into strips.

> Make a tomb out of a large appliance box.

> Make a stone covering for the entrance to the tomb out of posterboard or cardboard covered with table paper.

PROCEDURE
Ask a child to find information in the Searching Stop on burial customs.

Dress a child as Lazarus. Wrap him in strips of cloth, and put him in the tomb. (He must be able to bend.) Dress a child as Jesus. Dress two children as Mary and Martha.

Ask the large group to turn toward the tomb and listen to the report on burial customs. Ask, *Have you been to a funeral? What sounds do you remember? What smells do you remember? What do you remember seeing? In what ways do you miss those people who are now dead?* Present any of the following information[2] that was not covered in the report:

In biblical times, dead bodies were washed, and then oil was poured on them. Spices such as myrrh and aloe were used to make the body even cleaner and to make it smell better. The feet and hands were bandaged, the body was then wrapped in linen, and the face was covered with a separate cloth. Pass around a small sample of linen cloth. *Poor people had only very coarse linen.*

In biblical times, when someone died, a wail was given to announce what had happened. A wail was a loud scream, a sharp sound that was frightening. From the time someone died until he was buried, relatives and friends continued to wail and cry. Sometimes people were hired to continue this wailing. Ask a child to read Mark 5:38. *Often those who were sad tore their clothes and beat on their chests to show their sadness.* Ask a child to read 2 Samuel 3:31. *Mourners wore garments made from goats' hair. This material was called "sackcloth." It was rough and dark in color.*

It was a custom for relatives to fast, or not eat anything, until the dead person was buried. Luckily, people did not have to cry and wail and be hungry too long because the dead usually were buried on the day of their death. This was because the bodies began to decay, and the smell was terrible.

People were buried in tombs if they were wealthy. Tombs were similar to caves, but shelves intended for housing bodies were carved inside them. After a body was placed inside a tomb, a large stone was placed over the opening to protect the body. Ask a child to read Luke 24:1, 2. *If people were poor, they were usually buried in natural caves, whose openings also were covered by large stones.*

Plan cooperative Bible reading with the story of Lazarus. Ask the children to find John 11 in their Bibles. Say, *As I tell the story, I will ask you to read to yourselves a message found in certain verses and to tell us the message. I will also ask you to find the answers to some questions in certain verses.* Lead them as follows:

In the small town of Bethany, everyone was worried because Lazarus was sick. His sisters, Mary and Martha, did all they could for him, but Lazarus became even more sick. His sisters decided to send a message to Jesus, who was in Perea, across the Jordan River. In verse 3, read the message.

PERCEIVING

Mary, Martha, and Lazarus were some of Jesus' best friends, and he didn't want them to be sad. Nevertheless, he didn't go to them right away. Two days later Jesus and his friends left Perea for Bethany. "I'm going so that I can wake Lazarus out of his sleep," Jesus said. The disciples thought Lazarus was sleeping, but Jesus meant that Lazarus was already dead. Read what Jesus said to them in verse 14. Lazarus had been placed in a tomb instead of a cave, so perhaps Mary and Martha were not poor.

When the group reached Bethany, they found that Lazarus was already dead and buried. In verse 17, find out how long Lazarus had been buried.

The city of Jerusalem was only 2 miles away, so many believers from there had come to see Mary and Martha. But Martha was waiting for a special person to come. As soon as she heard that Jesus was near, she ran down the road to meet him. No doubt the two of them hugged each other. Then Martha said a strange thing. Find out what that was in verse 21.

"Your brother will rise from the dead," Jesus said to Martha. She answered him, "I know that he will rise again in the resurrection." Then Jesus said an amazing thing. In verses 25 and 26, read what he told Martha. Is this comforting to you? Martha did not completely understand it, but she was happy about it. She ran to tell her sister, Mary, that Jesus had come. Mary also came crying and met Jesus. A crowd of friends followed her. Then Jesus began to cry. Does this surprise you? Do you think Jesus had feelings just like we do?

Mary, Martha, and their friends took Jesus to Lazarus' tomb. A great stone covered the opening to the tomb. Then Jesus gave a command. Read it in verse 39. Why do you think Martha questioned the command?

Ask two children standing close by to roll the stone away from the opening. Remind them that it's very heavy. Ask Jesus to step forward and say, "I thank you, Father, for hearing my prayer," and then cry out in a loud voice, "Lazarus, come out." Lazarus will come out of the box. Ask Mary and Martha to come forward also. When Jesus says, "Unbind him and let him go," Mary and Martha will take the strips of cloth off him and embrace Lazarus. Then ask the group to read what happened next in verse 45. Ask, **Do you understand burial customs better now than before?** Help the children understand that God knows the hurt and grief of death and sent Jesus into this world to help people know how to live.

Talk to the children about making a faith commitment. Help them understand that because Lazarus was a believer, he would live forever, as Jesus said in verse 25. Explain what being a Christian means. Pray together that all of the children, at some time in their lives, will become believers and receive Jesus' promise to "live forever."

Synagogue Schools

RESOURCES
dowel sticks
paint
paper
pencils
pencil sharpener
school textbooks
"scrolls"
"wooden tablet"
"yarmulkes"

PREPARATION

> Sharpen dowel sticks to use for writing instruments.

> Ask several children to bring some of their school textbooks and show them to the group at the beginning of the session and talk about their favorite subjects.

PROCEDURE

Ask several children to go to the Searching Stop and prepare a report on synagogue schools.

In the center of the room, set up a synagogue class setting with several boys and a rabbi. They don't need costumes, but it will add greatly to the setting if they all are wearing yarmulkes (see p. 33). Provide scrolls (see pp. 21, 78) or wooden tablets (see p. 62) and writing instruments. Ask the other children to observe the setting.

Ask the children who have done research to present their reports. Present to the large group any of the following information[3] that was not given by the researchers:

Synagogue school was not a place where boys went to learn how to make a living. They went there to learn about their religious beliefs and history. Until about the age of 10, they studied the wonderful stories and history of the Jewish people. From age 10 to 15, they concentrated on Jewish law. Their textbook for all of this was the Old Testament, written on scrolls.

Boys began school at the age of 6 or 7 and went to the synagogue daily. At 12, a Jewish boy became a "son of the law." At age 13, he began his life's work in whatever trade he chose. See pp. 82, 83. *Boys were also expected to say from memory all the verses used in Temple services in Jerusalem. A Jewish boy was called a "son of the law" or a "son of the commandment" because, by age 13, he was supposed to know all of God's commandments. Also, sometime during his 13th year, a Jewish boy was expected to take part in the worship services at the Temple in Jerusalem.*

At school the boys sat cross-legged on the floor in a semicircle with the rabbi at the front. The rabbi was the leader or schoolmaster. He also sat cross-legged on the floor with a low desk in front of him on which he rested the scroll he taught from. When a boy

first attended school, he learned the Hebrew alphabet much as you learned your ABC's. Then, in Hebrew, the rabbi copied a passage that each child had learned at home and had said every day. This passage was probably Deuteronomy 6:4-5, known as the Shema. Ask all the children to copy this passage in English on sheets of paper. Ask them to roll their papers like scrolls. See p. 13.

The boys also learned the psalms and the words of the prophets. They knew the meaning behind all the Jewish festivals and celebrations. They wrote with reed pens on wooden tablets as well as on parchment scrolls. They probably learned some form of math. They took their lunches in leather bags called "scrips." Their lunches consisted of such foods as bread, cheese, and fruit.

Girls didn't go to school. They stayed home and learned from their mothers how to be wives and mothers. See p. 107.

Jesus went to synagogue school in Nazareth and then became a carpenter like his father. He studied year after year. In his grown-up life, he quoted many things he had learned in synagogue school. At what point in his life do you think he realized he was the promised Messiah the boys and their leader talked about so much in the synagogue school? Perhaps he knew it by the age of 12 when he was lost in the Temple and said to his mother, "I must be about my Father's business." Do you think so? See p. 88. *Do you think Jesus might be your best friend if you two were to attend the same school? Why?*

PERCEIVING

The Early Church at Worship

RESOURCES

cassette tape player
chalk
chalk/markerboard
felt tip pens
index cards (3"x5")
narrow ribbon
paper
taped song: "The God of Abraham Praise"
U.S. and/or world map

PREPARATION

> Display a U.S. and/or world map.

> Make a list of persons from your church who have left the community to share the gospel elsewhere. Obtain addresses and other information if needed.

PROCEDURE

Ask the children to name some places they see the word "Christian" other than in a church. They may say Christian radio, Christian school, Christian day care, bumper stickers, T-shirts, and so on. Ask, ***Do you remember any slogans you have seen with the word "Christian?" What do you think of this way of witnessing about your faith? When you see or hear the word "Christian," what is the first thing you think of?*** List responses on chalk/markerboard or paper. Use them to put together a definition of Christian. Write it so all can see.

Ask, ***Who were the early Christians?*** Explain that they were called "Christians" because they lived right after the death of Jesus. Say, ***The early Christians tried to meet in synagogues to worship, but they were badly mistreated, so they began meeting in other places. Where? Find the answer in 1 Corinthians 16:19, Colossians 4:15, Philemon 2, and Acts 5:42.*** They met in homes and ate together. ***They also went to the Temple every day. In their meetings they talked about the things they remembered about Jesus. Some remembered*** his stories, others talked about how he had healed people, and others could not forget some of his wise sayings.

Ask the children to name some places where Christians meet today if they do not have church buildings. They may say: store buildings, trailer parks, homes, office buildings, tents, African huts, and schools.

Say, ***Look in your Bibles in Ephesians 5:18-20 to see how Paul encouraged the Christians of the first century to praise God in their worship services. In verse 19, find a phrase that tells how they took Paul's advice and praised God.*** They sang psalms, hymns, and spiritual songs. ***They worshiped in much the same way as we do. They enjoyed being together. They observed the Lord's Supper, baptized, prayed, and sang. They also listened to sermons and collected offerings. Many people believe that Paul's letters were read in churches and became part of the worship services. The people also read passages from the Old Testament.***

People in the early church helped others. Widows could not earn a living in that time, so they had to be taken care of. Children without parents could not take care of themselves either. Sometimes hungry people in churches far away needed money for food. There was unexpected suffering and trouble. People needed help then just as they do today. Early church Christians were missionaries. Ask a leader to read aloud Acts 4:32, 34. ***Special persons were chosen to help others. Read Acts 6:1-7 to find out how many of these people there were. What are they called in our churches today?*** Deacons.

The early Christians made some changes in their worship. Because Jesus rose from the grave on the first day of the week, they decided to make Sunday the day to worship in public rather than Saturday, the Jewish day of

worship. Some people in the early church chanted scripture verses. Would you like to do some chanting? Stand as the early Christians did.

Divide the children into three groups. Give the following assignments:

Group 1: "Praise the Lord."
Group 2: "Praise, praise, praise."
Group 3: "Give thanks."

Instruct all groups to speak at the same time, saying their words repeatedly. Caution against groups trying to outchant others. As they speak, a leader reads Psalm 150. When the leader closes her Bible, that is the signal for everyone to stop.

Say, *After Jesus' death there was much persecution, meaning the Christians were treated very badly by people who didn't understand who Jesus was. Some Christians were killed, some were jailed, and some were beaten. They faced illness and separation. And yet in the book of Acts, the book that tells about the early church, the word joy is used 8 times. The early Christians also had a secret emblem that identified them. It was in the shape of a fish. Wherever they went, they could find each other with this sign. Because of the persecution, they began to leave Jerusalem and go other places. As they did, they carried the message of Jesus with them, even to other races of people. We could compare their telling the message of Jesus in many places to farmers scattering seed.*

The following activity will help the children realize the far-reaching witness of their own church. Ask the children to write on index cards the first and last names and cities, states, and countries of those people from your church/group who have left the community and are telling the good news in other places. Include seminary and college students, pastors, missionaries, leaders, lay

people and church staff who have moved away, chaplains, men and women in military service, and church members temporarily displaced. Supplement the information if needed. Place the cards on the wall/board around the map. Attach narrow ribbon from the cards to the place on the map where those persons are. Ask, *Will you write encouraging notes to these people? Can you be filled with joy in difficult times? How?*

Play "The God of Abraham Praise," a traditional Hebrew melody (see p. 174). Ask the children to give this Jewish farewell to each other: "Peace be with you." Each child answers: "And also with you."

Notes

[1]Adapted from Fred H. Wight, *Manners and Customs of Bible Lands* (Chicago: Moody Press, 1953) 7-9.

[2]Adapted from *Jesus and His Times* (Pleasantville NY: Reader's Digest Assoc., Inc., 1987) 116-17.

[3]Information on synagogue schools adapted from Betty Goetz and Ruthe Bomberger, *Marketplace, 29 A.D., A Bible Times Experience* (Stevensville MI: B. J. Goetz Publishing Co., 1989) 140; and Marion C. Armstrong, *Home Life in Bible Times* (Nashville: Abingdon Press, 1943) 5.

Chapter 4
SIMULATING: Experiencing Adventure Through Drama

Rationale

Most children love to act, pretend, or imitate. In education circles, this is known as simulating. Most of us use the words drama or playacting. Drama is not an exhibition or display, although the use of actors and costumes and props helps provide a realistic atmosphere. Rather, it is leaving oneself for a few minutes and experiencing an adventure. It's a wonderful way to transport children mentally back into biblical times and places. Drama should not be hurried, and likewise, it does not have to include continuous motion. It could involve Daniel posed beside his vegetables and water, or objects placed as still life to create a mood.

Through the different types of dramatic activities described in this chapter children are taught cooperation, research skills, problem solving, the ability to analyze and think critically, and application of biblical truths in their lives. Following the dramatic activities are detailed suggestions for making costumes. (Suggestion: Do not use costumes until the last session so as to maintain the children's interest and attention.)

Plays

RESOURCES
costumes
scenery
props
sound effects

PREPARATION
> Study carefully the story that is to be presented.

PROCEDURE
Discuss the story with the children. Establish the characters and scene. Talk about why the people acted as they did in the story. Talk about some of the problems, needs, and admirable qualities of the characters. Look at pictures to learn about the clothing and background of the time.

Assign actors. Allow children to decide on their own dialogue and also where to stop the action. Don't ask them to memorize "parts." Ask them to think of a time when they, too, felt the same way.

For persons who do not wish to act, assign tasks such as choosing taped background music; preparing background scenery, sound effects, and props; and putting away costumes. (Examples of sound effects: a hairdryer to produce the sound of wind; a tone block and a stick to make the sound of someone walking; the sound of money dropping into a plate; recorded effects of someone throwing rocks, hammering, laughing, rattling a big piece of tin for thunder).

During large group time, position 2 or 3 groups of children at different stations in the room. Each group will take turns presenting different parts in the story. Focus the viewers' attention on these groups at different points in the story.

Or, station a Bible character in the background who listens to what is being said. She may choose to comment at some point. Following are some suggested stories:

- *Blind Bartimaus* (Mark 10:46-52). Blindfold the actor before taking him to another spot in the building. Leave him for awhile. He can't take the blindfold off, but instead, he must listen to the people walking by and ask for alms. When he returns to the group, he describes his feelings.

- *Triumphal entry of Jesus into Jerusalem* (John 12:12-18). Form a procession outside the building or down the hall. Ask other groups to come and watch. Provide palm trees and branches (see p. 96) and a real or "pretend" donkey or colt.

- *Dialogue between King Xerxes I and Haman* (Esther 6). Station 6 children in pairs around the room with their backs to the large group. Each pair is engaged in conversation. Show the children the name of King Xerxes I (Ahasuerus) in an encyclopedia, and read about him.

- *Naomi and Ruth* (see Ruth 1, 2). Ask these characters to stand in the center of the room and chat. Ask 4 or 5 children to act as town gossips and cluster in several different areas of the room. Occasionally, they turn around to look at Ruth, the newcomer.

Minidramas

RESOURCES
costumes
scenery
props
sound effects

PREPARATION
> Decide on stories or situations to present.

PROCEDURE
At the beginning of a session, present a problem or an idea for group discussion or to explain a

truth. Following each presentation, discuss the lesson to be learned from it. Give all children the opportunity to express their feelings. Following are some suggested situations:

- Dress a child as King Nebuchadnezzar (see p. 32) Ask him, **Why did you insist that your people worship a 90' gold statue?**

- Dress a child as Pharaoh (see p. 33). Ask her, **Should you kill Moses just because Moses killed someone else?** To encourage discussion from the rest of the group, ask, **How does Pharaoh's method of punishment, as shown in this story, compare to today's court system?**

- Provide an apron, schoolbooks, and a jacket for Stephanie. Explain the situation to the group: **Stephanie has just walked in the door from school. Her mother is not very happy. Wearing an apron, Mom meets Stephanie at the door. Instead of saying, "Hi," she begins to talk about what Stephanie has not done. She did not feed the dog this morning, make her bed, or hang up her clothes.** Ask 2 children to act out the conversation and demonstrate how Stephanie's mother could reprimand her kindly.

- Provide a doll, a policeman's cap, a driver's license, a speeding ticket, and a pencil. Explain the situation to the group: **A family is in the car going on vacation. The children are in the back seat. The father is speeding. A policeman stops him and gives him a ticket.** Discuss what the conversation might be after the policeman leaves.

Pantomime

RESOURCES
costumes
scenery
props
sound effects

PREPARATION
> Decide on stories or situations to present.

PROCEDURE

As you read a passage from the Bible or a modern-day book or tell a story, ask children to pantomime the action. Present a problem or situation. Ask children to pantomime a solution. Ask others in the group to guess what the solution is. Talk about the story or situation until the children are very familiar with the feelings of the characters. Following the presentation, discuss the lesson to be learned from it. Following are some suggested situations:

• Provide a man's shirt and necktie, a pair of glasses, a mustache, a lady's purse, a pair of high heel shoes, a lady's wig, a tube of lipstick, some jewelry, children's dress-up clothes, a Bible for each person, and offering envelopes. Arrange chairs in the shape of car seats. Make 4 tires from posterboard or use the tires you have in the room (see p. 9). Lean tires against the chairs on 4 corners. Explain the situation: *A family is in the car on the way to church. They are very late. The father blames the mother for being late, and the mother blames the children.* Ask some children to pantomime the argument. Ask the group to guess what the story is about. Then guide discussion of these questions: *How could these things be said without anger? Has your family ever had this conversation?* Ask for other comments on the situation.

• Prior to the session, read the book of Philemon. Present the story of Paul, Onesimus, and Philemon to the children. Guide the children to present the story in pantomime. Suggested scenes are: Onesimus running away, Paul and Onesimus, Paul writing to Philemon, Philemon accepting Onesimus. Stop the action. Ask, *Whose head was hanging down? Who encouraged someone in the story to apologize? What do you think happened next?* Allow the actors to finish the story in pantomime.

• Tell the story of a shipwreck (Acts 27). Ask several children to pantomime how they would react to a terrible storm at sea. Talk about the importance of cooperation for survival. Ask several children to

stand close together with their backs to each other. Tie a rope around their waists. Ask each child to try to go in a different direction. Then ask the children to move to a destination in the room, working together to get there. Ask, *What happened? Why was cooperation necessary in this Bible story?*[1]

• Designate 3 places in the room. Label them Antioch, Cyprus, and Iconium. As you tell the story of Paul and Barnabus' missionary travels (Acts 13–15), ask the costumed actors to move silently on cue from one place to another. Or tell the story of Lydia. Label 3 areas in the room Philippi, Lydia's house, and the river. Say, *And now we go to the river for the next part of the story.* Talk about the 2 stories with the large group.

• When studying a unit on family life, ask some children to act out silently ways to help at home, using the supplies you have in the room: a garbage can, a sink, an ironing board, pillows, chairs, and rugs. Allow the other children to guess what each action is.

• Read a Bible verse. Ask a child to pantomime what that verse means to her.

Dramatic Interviews

RESOURCES

optional costumes
scenery
props
sound effects

PREPARATION

> Decide on stories and situations to present.

> Print a list of interview questions.

PROCEDURE

Ask the children to watch actual TV newscasts to see how reporters interview persons. Ask them to note how long the interviews last and whether the questioners use notes or rely on their memories. Explain that those who are being interviewed must know the facts of the story well. Assign materials to be read and studied. Give the children a list of questions that will be asked in the interview. Following are some suggested situations:

- In the large group time, give the children an opportunity to interview the 12 disciples. You may want to dress only a few children in costume to represent all of the 12. Ask them questions such as these: **When you began to see the miracles, could you believe what you were seeing? Why do you think some people never became Jesus' followers?**

- In small group time, ask the children and leaders to review the story of Pentecost in Acts 2. Then let one costumed child interview the larger group of children as they pretend to have been present when Peter preached his famous sermon and 3,000 people were added to the group of believers. The interviewer might ask questions such as, "You were there. What did you see?" Interview 2 early church Christians in the Pentecost crowd. Allow them to talk about the dangers they faced (see Acts 7:54-60; 8:1-3; 12:1-5).

Dramatic Readings

RESOURCES
copies of readings
highlight markers

PREPARATION
> Make copies of the dialogue found in a Bible story. In different colors, highlight the words of the characters to be portrayed.

PROCEDURE
Assign characters and a narrator (reads the verses between dialogue lines). Distribute copies of readings. Following are some suggested situations:

- The healing of a blind man in Bethsaida (Mark 8:22-26)
- Jesus stills a storm (Mark 4:35-41)
- The rich young ruler (Matthew 19:16-30)

Role-Plays

RESOURCES
optional costumes
scenery
props
sound effects

PREPARATION
> Decide on situations or problems to present.

PROCEDURE
Name the situation and talk about it. Let the children choose roles, but lead them to choose roles that do not describe themselves. (That way, they won't get too involved with the acting to see solutions!) Review the situation again. Set the scene. Give the children a minute or two to think about and "feel" the role. Allow the children to decide what they want to say and to express their own feelings. Ask questions about the situation. Discuss the outcomes. Have children switch roles and act out the situation again. Discontinue the activity when you think solutions are exhausted. Discuss with the children what they learned about problem solving. Following are some suggested situations:

- Jealousy between Saul and David (1 Samuel 18:6-16)
- The faith of a deaf-mute whom Jesus healed (Mark 7:31-37)
- The stoning of Stephen (Acts 7:54-60)

Picture Poses

RESOURCES
optional costumes
scenery
props
sound effects

PREPARATION
> Decide on scenes, set both in biblical as well as contemporary times.

PROCEDURE

Assign children to pretend to be the characters in a picture or a scene, assuming the positions and expressions of the characters. They do not move or speak. Following are some suggested situations:

- Samuel's call (1 Samuel 3:1-21)
- Jesus calls four fishermen (Matthew 4:18-22)
- The man with a paralyzed hand (Matthew 12:9-14)

Tableaus

RESOURCES
optional costumes
scenery
props
sound effects

PREPARATION

> Decide on scenes, both from biblical as well as contemporary times.

PROCEDURE

Ask children to pose without moving throughout most of the scene. Occasionally an actor can step out of the scene to say something. They will step forward to speak and then retreat back into their poses. Following are some suggested situations:

- Noah building the ark (Genesis 6:1-22)
- Jesus in the temple (Luke 2:39-50)
- The rich young man (Matthew 19:16-22)

Making Costumes

RESOURCES
bathrobes
bedsheets
bias tape
boots
braid
burlap
cardboard
carpet scraps
construction paper (brown, black, gray)
cord or twill tape or thin rope
costume jewelry
curtains
fabric (different kinds/colors/sizes)
fake fur (brown, black, gray)
felt tip pens
fringe
grocery bags (paper)
masking tape
"moneybag"
muslin material
needles
paint (black)
paintbrushes (small)
paper grocery bags
pinking shears
posterboard
rags
rope
sewing machine
scissors
snaps
spray paint or foil (gold, silver)
staples
stapler
"sword"
thread
trims
twill tape (from an upholstery shop)

PREPARATION

> Search fabric stores for inexpensive remnant fabrics and trims.

> Ask seamstresses for leftover fabric.

> Purchase costume materials at garage sales and thrift stores.

> Enlist help to make costumes.

Woman's headpiece

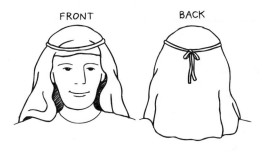

FRONT

BACK

Man's headpiece

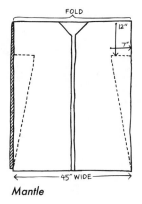

FOLD

12"

7"

45" WIDE

Mantle

PROCEDURE

To make simple costumes: (1) Drape a long piece of fabric around an actor's shoulders. (2) Use a bathrobe. (3) Draw around a child while he is lying on a sheet of posterboard. Cut out the face and armhole areas. Draw on the posterboard a costume for the character. The child holds the poster in front of him as he speaks. (4) Use large paper grocery bags with holes cut out for the arms. Draw on a costume.

All Jews wore a girdle (belt), a headpiece, an outer robe called a mantle or cloak, sandals or shoes, and a tunic. Although Jewish clothing was usually made of linen or wool, for children's costumes, use inexpensive fabric of a natural color or dyed blue, brown, pink, crimson, or purple; or use striped material or discarded bedsheets. For the wealthier citizens, use richer-looking fabric and trims. For beggars, lepers, prodigals, and the demon-possessed, use burlap or another rough fabric that is torn, dirty, and patched. These characters would probably be barefoot. (Lepers usually had rags wound around their skin to hide the marks of leprosy.) Make the following articles of Jewish clothing:

- *Girdle*: Cut fabric pieces 3" wide and 63" long. Tie around the waist. Or cut the hems off the ends of discarded bedsheets. Attach a money bag (see p. 32) and/or a sword (see p. 14).

- *Headpiece*: Cut women's headpieces 1⅓ yards long and 18" wide. Wear as shown. Cut men's headpieces 36" x 36". Fold into a triangle. Place the point at the center back and the longest side across the forehead as shown. Tie with rope around the forehead, knotting it in the back.

- *Mantle*: Cut 45" fabric open all the way down the front. Place the point of the sleeve 7" over from the outer edge and 12" down from the shoulder seam. Stitch on the outside. Do not turn fabric. Or, turn a discarded bedsheet wrongside out and fold in half, leaving the fold on one side. Stitch a shoulder seam.

Cut a hole for the head. Turn fabric to the right side. Stitch. Do not turn fabric inside out or cut out excess fabric. Slit all the way down the side that has a fold.

- *Sandals*: On thick carpet scraps draw around children's' feet. Cut out patterns. Attach twill tape or cord to the soles, and wind it around the feet and ankles. Make a thong across the front of the sandals.

- *Tunic*: Measure several children from their necks to the tops of their feet to get an average length. Double measurement. Use 43" fabric for authentic-looking tunics. Use 36" fabric for simple-looking tunics. Fold fabric in half evenly, with the fold at the top. At the top front of the costume, cut a hole just large enough to slip the tunic over a child's head. To make sleeves, place the point of the sleeve 8" over from the outer edge and 11" down from the shoulder seam. Do not turn costume inside out after stitching. Do not cut out excess fabric. Stitch on the side of the fabric you wish to show. Taper side seams of the tunic. Sew a small stitch close to the outer edge of fabric, or use pinking shears when cutting the fabric. Masking tape could be used on the wrong side to hold a temporary hem or to repair a hem.

Make other costume items:

- *Babylonian clothing*: Make a tunic. Attach decorative braid to the bottom of the sleeves and to the neck. Make a belt (girdle) for the waist out of the tunic fabric. Tie a piece of the same fabric around the head.

- *Beard*: Cut a 3½" x 12" piece of brown, black, or gray construction paper. Cut vertical strips across the bottom within ½" of the top of paper. Curl the beard by pulling each strip between your thumb and the blades of metal scissors. Attach behind the ears. Or cut a piece of fake fur 10" across the top and 6" long. Cut a slit for the mouth. Sew on ribbon tapes. Tie the beard around the head.

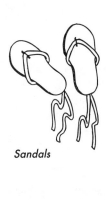

Sandals

Simple tunic

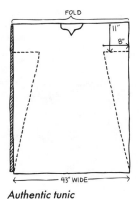

Authentic tunic

Babylonian clothing

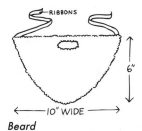

Beard

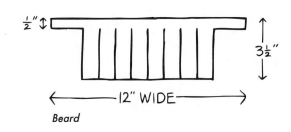

Beard

A Roman Soldier

Breastplate

Egyptian clothing

Helmet

Nebuchadnezzar's crown

- *Breastplate*: To make a breastplate, cut the shape for the front and back from 2 large paper grocery bags. Use tape to fasten the sides together. Spray paint silver. Draw details with black paint and a small brush. Or cut the shape for the front and back from silver fabric. Draw the details with black paint. Complete the costume by adding a short "skirt" and boots.

- *Crown*: Cut from cardboard. Cover with gold foil or gold spray paint.

- *Egyptian clothing*: For women, make a tunic and belt. Cut muslin doubled in the shape of the collar. Stitch. Turn to the right side. Make jewel decorations using colorful felt tip pens. Complete the outfit with gold costume jewelry bracelets or bracelets made from gold foil. For men, make a "skirt." Make a collar from muslin. Make jewel decorations using colorful felt tip pens. Attach snaps to the back of the collar. Fasten collar. Complete the outfit with gold costume jewelry bracelets or bracelets made from gold foil.

- *Helmet*: Mold a paper bag into the appropriate shape. Staple. Spray paint silver.

- *Money bags*: Cut pieces of burlap 4½" x 5½". Include a 1¼" casing turned down at the top for the cord to go through. Fold casing over at the top. Stitch. Thread cording through the casing to make a drawstring.

- *Nebuchadnezzar's crown*: Cut from posterboard. Mold into the correct shape. Fasten with masking tape. Spray paint gold. Decorate with a brown felt tip pen.

- *Pharaoh's headdress*: Cut from posterboard. Fasten with masking tape. Or, use a large grocery bag. Spray paint gold. Draw narrow black lines. Or, use gold and black striped fabric.

- *Prayer shawl*: Cut a piece of cotton, wool, or silk 10″ wide and 80″ long. Attach fringe on the two ends. Or, draw fringe and stripes with a felt tip pen.

- *Rope tie for headpiece*: Cut thin rope into 38″ lengths. Burn the ends with a match. Knot rope in back of the head.

- *Yarmulke*: Cut dark material into 6 strips of 3½″ x 5″ each. Sew together with ¼″ seams. Bind around the edges with bias tape.

Note

¹Teaching method adapted from and reprinted by permission of TEACH Newsletter (Summer 1993) 7. TEACH may be obtained from 3950 Fossil Creek Blvd., Suite 201, Ft. Worth TX 76137.

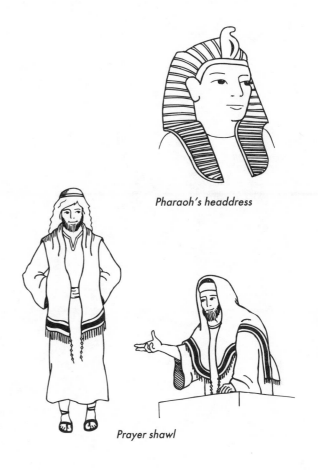

Pharaoh's headdress

Prayer shawl

Yarmulke

SIMULATING

Chapter 5
PONDERING: Relating Feelings to Bible Characters

Rationale

Nancy Hanks

If Nancy Hanks came back as a ghost,
Seeking news of what she loved most,
She'd ask first,
Where's my son?
What's happened to Abe?
What's he done?

Poor little Abe
Left all alone
Except for Tom,
Who's a rolling stone;
He was only nine
The year I died.
I remember still
How hard he cried.

Scraping along
In a little shack
With hardly a shirt
To cover his back.
And a prairie wind
To blow him down,
Or pinching times
If he went to town.

You wouldn't know
About my son?
Did he grow tall?
Did he have fun?
Did he learn to read?
Did he get to town?
Do you know his name?
Did he get on?

A Reply to Nancy Hanks

Yes, Nancy Hanks
The news we will tell
Of your Abe
Whom you loved so well.
You asked first
Where's my son?
He lives in the heart of everyone.[1]

Have you ever read a poem with more feeling? A young mother dies too soon. She is not around to watch her son grow up, to share in the exciting times in his life, or to witness his inauguration as President of the United States. In this poem, we also see the feelings of the young Abe Lincoln, age 9.

God gave us feelings. Some are hard to handle. Children have feelings that baffle, bewilder, and burden. A leader said to a child, "We missed you last Sunday." He replied, "I was at my dad's." "Did you have a fun weekend?" the leader said. "No," he replied, "didn't want to go. Judge says I have to."

Children of today live under stress of all kinds. We must help them understand that Bible persons lived under stress, too, and they didn't always make wise decisions. Though I have used the names of certain Bible characters throughout the book, the activities are by no means confined to those persons. The feeling, thinking, and creative writing activities can be used to teach about other Bible personalities as well.

Feeling Activities

DISCOURAGEMENT
(Acts 3:1-11)

RESOURCES
paper
pencils
3 costumes (1 ragged)

PREPARATION
> Assign children to role-play the lame man and 2 helpers.

PROCEDURE

Dress a child as a lame man in a ragged costume. Ask 2 costumed children to take the lame man and lay him at a main entrance to the building to ask for alms while you lead in the following activity.

Instruct the other children to hop on 1 foot, turn around 3 times, stand in one spot while marching, and jump up and down. Say, **There is just one problem with doing all this. You can't walk.** Ask the children and leaders to sit on the floor. Make it clear that they cannot get up. Say, **You aren't _____ or _____; you're the lame man. Imagine being like this for the rest of your life! What are some things you can't do?** Continue with questions. Give the children a chance to respond.

How long have you been crippled? Do you have a home? If you can't walk, how do you get here? Why do you sit here instead of someplace else? What are you asking people to give you? Can you get alms (money) some other way? Do you think people like you, or do they give you coins because they feel sorry for you? Does it make you feel somehow less important than others because you have to beg? Are there many beggars like you? Are there any doctors anywhere who can make you well?

When you saw Peter and John coming for the 3 o'clock prayer time at the Temple, you asked them for alms. What did Peter say when you asked him for money? Did you think you could do it? You had been crippled all your life. What part of your body suddenly became strong? Who are you going to thank for this? How do you think Peter and John were able to do this miracle? Do you think you made a spectacle of yourself by jumping and leaping, or were you so happy you just couldn't help it? Who was looking on when it happened? When you left home this morning, did you even dream you would have this kind of a day? If you had never been to the Temple, what

would you have learned about it from this story? Peter gave quite a sermon. The Temple was large, and lots of people passed by. How did they hear him without a microphone?

Ask the 2 children in costume to go after the child portraying the lame man, bring him in, and lay him on the floor. Hand out paper and pencils. Ask the children to write 2 or 3 sentences about how they feel at the present. Give them a chance to comment on the satisfying outcome for the lame man and for Peter and John. Ask the lame man what was the response of the people he saw. Did he get any coins?

LONELINESS

(John 10:1-18)

RESOURCES

Bible or musical arrangement of Psalm 23
"campfire"
flashlight or "oil lamp"
masking tape
red cellophane paper
"shepherd's staff"
"stones"

PREPARATION

> In a corner of the room mark off a fenced area with masking tape. Make a doorway in it.

> In the center of the room, make a campfire with stones (see p. 71).

> Place a shepherd's staff (see p. 13) near the campfire.

PROCEDURE

Appoint several children to be a fence, some to be sheep, some to be evil shepherds, and one child to be the good shepherd. Ask the children and leaders to sit on the floor around the campfire. Darken the room. Use a flashlight or an oil lamp to refer to the Bible. Give the following introduction:

Have you ever felt all alone, as if there were no one else in the whole world but you? The life of a shepherd was a lonely one. It was really dark. Shepherds could see only by the light of a campfire. It was hot during the day and cold at night. It could be boring or frightening watching sheep all day and night. Sometimes the shepherds spent days and weeks out in the field.

Shepherds had to take very good care of sheep. The sheep often drank poisoned water, and they couldn't fight back against wild animals. They wandered into dangerous places. The sheep could drown because their coats got heavy when wet. A shepherd's staff with a crook on top lifted the sheep up and out. Show the staff. *At night the shepherds checked each sheep for briars and thistles and put oil on the heads of the sheep. Then the shepherds herded them into pens for safety. The pens had 1 gate, and a shepherd slept by the gate to guard it. Each shepherd knew his own sheep, and each sheep knew its shepherd's voice and followed only him. Jesus once compared himself to a shepherd and called us his "sheep." Can you understand why?* [2]

Turn on the lights. Ask the children to turn toward the fenced area. *A long time ago the shepherds built fences around their fields. The fences had no doors. The good shepherd sat in the doorway to count, care for, and protect the sheep.* The good shepherd and sheep enter. *This was because the bad shepherds wanted to bother and hurt and sometimes steal the sheep.* The evil shepherds enter. *But the sheep did not even listen to them.* The sheep ignore the bad shepherds. *Jesus said, "I am the door, and if you come in this way, you will be protected." Remember, Jesus came as a shepherd to look after his sheep—you and me.* [3]

Ask, *What do you think Jesus meant by this verse: "I am the gate for the sheep"? Or by this verse: "I am the good shepherd. The good*

shepherd lays down his life for the sheep?" What does this sentence mean: "I am the good shepherd; I know my own, and my own know me?" Do we ever need to feel lonely with God as our shepherd? Here is a song a lonely shepherd once wrote. Listen to it, and think about how God takes care of us. Read Psalm 23 or play a musical arrangement of it.

FEAR
(Exodus 3, 4)

RESOURCES
"animals"
backdrop of sheep figures
"bushes" or "shrubs"
costume for Moses
construction paper
dialogue copies
large piece of paper
newspapers
"sandy floor"
"stones"
walking stick

PREPARATION
> Move room furnishings to the wall.

> Transform the room into a desert in Midian.

> Arrange a lot of stones and a few fake bushes or shrubs.

> Ask a small group of children to draw on table paper a sandy floor, some desert animals that might be crawling there (for example, snakes

and scorpions), and some ridges in the sand. Or, make the animals from newspaper-stuffed construction paper shapes, stapled around the edges to hold both sides together.

> Place the backdrop of the sheep (see p. 12) low on the wall.

> Attach a large piece of paper on the wall beside the classroom door. Write the word "MOSES" at the top.

> Make copies of the dialogue below:

God: Moses, I'm the God of your fathers. I want you to go to Egypt and get my people out of there.

Moses: I don't mean to be disrespectful, God, but surely you don't mean that. As you remember, I left there, and not under very good circumstances. I killed a man. That's definitely not the place for me to go back to.

God: I'm going to send you anyway.

Moses: Why me?

God: Because I'm going to do surprising things in Egypt, and you're going to talk to Pharaoh for me.

Moses: But what if he doesn't listen to me?

God: See that walking stick in your hand? Throw it down. Now you see that it becomes a snake. Reach down and pick it up by the tail. You can see that it is your walking stick again. Put your hand inside your robe. (Moses obeys, puts his hand inside his robe, draws it out, and looks at it strangely.) Now you see that it is a leper's hand. Put it back in. (Moses puts his hand in his robe, takes it out again, and it looks normal.)

Moses: Oh, man, I've never been a good speaker. Can't you just send somebody else?

God: I'll be with you and tell you everything to say.

PROCEDURE

As the children arrive, ask them to write on the paper a few words that describe Moses.

Dress Moses in costume. Have him sit with a walking stick in his hand. Give him a copy of the dialogue. Ask a leader to be the voice of God coming from another part of the room. Give him a copy of the dialogue.

Ask, *What would Moses think about during the hours and hours he had alone with the sheep in Midian? He probably thought about a bad mistake he had made many years before. If Moses lived in the present, the conversation might go something like this.* The leader and child speak the dialogue.

Say, *Moses changed his mind. He decided to do exactly what God asked him to. Moses was a missionary. In what ways did Moses feel he was handicapped? Why didn't he just give up? What qualities does Moses display that you didn't know he had? Do you know a real-life person who hasn't given up when times were hard?*

How do you feel when you hear the word "earthquake?" Are you frightened? Can you get a sense of how Moses felt when God gave him this hard job to do? Can you tremble all over to demonstrate how you feel?

Can you express some thoughts Moses must have had earlier in the story when he killed the Egyptian? In spite of his "handicaps," what traits did Moses have that God could use? We know from history books that a boy growing up in Egypt would have learned reading, writing, math, geometry, trigonometry, astronomy, architecture, chemistry, science, and music.[4]

Ask, *Why did Moses deserve a pat on the back? Would you have had his kind of courage? What if God were to call you to do a very difficult thing?* Discuss modern-day people who have faced difficult tasks. Ask, *If you were an artist, what would you draw into a picture on this incident?*

COMPASSION
(Luke 10:30-35)

RESOURCES
pieces of paper
"road"
"stones"

PREPARATION
> Draw a road on paper that stretches from one end of the room to the other. Place it on the floor along with lots of "stones" (see p. 14).

> Write on pieces of paper the names of characters in the story.

PROCEDURE
Say, *Turn in your Bibles to Luke 10:30-35. Help me picture the scene. Many priests who served in the Temple lived in Jericho. It is one of the oldest known towns in the world—probably 11,000 years old.*[5] *It was hot and sun-baked and a winter vacation place for the wealthy. There were many palm trees. A modern-day traveler can see bananas, papayas, oranges, and grapefruits there. What is meant by "down" to Jericho in verse 30?* The road from Jerusalem to Jericho drops 3,000 feet over a span of 15 miles.[6] *Jerusalem was the most important city in the world to the Jewish people. That was where the Temple stood. Who do you suppose traveled this road from Jerusalem to Jericho?* It was lonely, rocky, and deserted.

Ask each child to read the Bible passage silently. Say, *Tell me which of these persons does not appear in the story: a soldier, a tax collector, a Levite, a priest, a "certain man," a seller of purple cloth, robbers, an innkeeper, a Samaritan.*

Distribute pieces of paper with the names of characters who are in the story. The children are to pretend to be the people on their papers. Give the "pretenders" a couple minutes to consider the reasons behind their actions, and then to report to the rest of the group.

Say, *The priest and the Levite both served God in the Temple. They ignored the wounded man for fear of defiling themselves, or being spiritually unclean and temporarily unfit to help in the Temple. For all they knew, he was dead, and they would become even more unclean by touching a dead body.*

In biblical times, Jews and Samaritans were not friends. And yet, prejudice is forgotten in this story as one man helps another. A denarii was 1 day's wages. But the Samaritan gave the innkeeper 2 days' wages. What do you suppose the Samaritan and the wounded man talked about on the way to the inn?

Help the children understand that this may be either a true story or just one of Jesus' parables—a short, imaginary story that teaches a lesson. Ask, *What is the best thing we can learn from this parable?*

FORGIVENESS/UNFORGIVENESS
(1 Samuel 17:57; 18:1-9; 24:1-15)

RESOURCES
cassette tape player
dates
"girdle"
large appliance box
"slingshot"
"sword"
taped harp music

PREPARATION
> Purchase dates for children to eat.

> Make a girdle (see p. 30), a slingshot (see p. 13), and a sword (see p. 14).

PONDERING

PROCEDURE

Dress a child as David, with a sword and a sling-shot hanging from his girdle. Hide David inside the box before the other children enter the room.

Have the large group face the appliance box. Ask, *What did David have in his hand the first time he met Saul? Look it up in 1 Samuel 17:57. Do you think that was pretty impressive? If you drew a picture of Saul and David standing together, who would look older, be taller, be smiling? How did David feel about Saul? How did Saul feel about David? How did David and Jonathan feel about each other?*

Ask a child to tell briefly the story of how Saul became jealous of David. See 1 Samuel 18:7-9. Say, *Saul then was determined to kill David. What is the real danger in anger and jealousy?* Ask a child to come forward and assume a position of anger. Ask, *Is this how Saul must have looked many times? It's normal to have revengeful feelings. The key is to get rid of them as soon as possible and replace them with good feelings.*

Play some taped harp music for the children. Ask, *Can you see how this music might have quieted King Saul? Why? Was there a better way David and Saul could have handled their conflict? Do you remember from the story that Saul was mind-sick and had supreme authority as king? How would you like to run from an enemy for 7 years? David ran from King Saul that long. Many of us feel mistreated sometimes, but we don't have enemies who are trying to kill us. What was the constant struggle in David's mind?*

Once David hid in caves at En-gedi. You'll remember it was there that, rather than killing Saul, he cut off a corner of his robe. En-gedi is a place of huge mountains and caves. It's an oasis between Jericho and

Masada. Date palms grow there. To help us remember En-gedi and David's experience, we're going to eat some dates.

Bring David out of the cave to eat and talk with the children. He might talk about how much he would like to go home and could teach the children to use a slingshot (in a safe place). Say, *David wasn't even happy when his enemy died. Can you imagine that? If you could choose one character in this story as your best friend, who would you choose? Is there a lesson you can learn from the story of King Saul? What about this? Be careful how you choose your leaders. "But," you are thinking, "lots of people followed King Saul. He was their hero, and they were his disciples." What is a disciple? Could you be a disciple of someone who would lead you into trouble? Kirby was a gang leader whom others followed into trouble. Now he is a disciple of Jesus. He is a real person who has been ordained as a minister in prison and witnesses to other inmates. What kind of person would you prefer to follow?*

PREJUDICE
(Book of Esther)

RESOURCES
background music
"gold goblets"
grapes
melons
Oriental rug (small)
pillows
table
tablecloth
tambourine

PREPARATION
> Move furnishings away from the center of the room.

> Set up the space as a banquet room in the palace of King Ahasuerus.

> Place melons, a cluster of grapes, and gold goblets on a table covered with a cloth.

> Place a small Oriental rug on the floor. Scatter pillows around.

> Cover a chair with red fabric to use as a throne.

PROCEDURE

Dress characters in costumes befitting their roles. Seat Esther in the banquet hall. Seat the king and Haman on either side of Esther. Play background music and a tambourine. Ask servants to offer grapes and melon to the guests.

Ask, *In what ways are people different from each other?* The children may suggest: fat/thin; skin color; handicapped or not; educated/uneducated; rich/poor; the way we dress; clean/dirty; attractive/unattractive. Display the word prejudice. Ask, *What does this word mean?* Listen for responses. *Could it also mean to "look down on" or to feel that we are "better than"? Help me think of some people we tend to look down on.* Children may suggest: handicapped, a brilliant person, other races, blind or mentally retarded, the elderly, prison inmates, certain religious groups, the opposite sex, persons who are addicted. Ask, *Have you ever felt left out of a group? Have you ever heard the statement "They're all alike" to describe a group? We call that "labeling." In the story today, Haman did not like Jews because he did not like Mordecai. Mordecai was different. Haman was labeling.*

To help the children get the feel of prejudice, ask them to form a circle. Say, *Join hands. Your object is to keep _____ from getting into the circle by making the chain strong enough. _____ will try for 1 minute.* The child pushes very hard. Those in the circle move closer to each other so there is no space open to him. He tries everything, including going between their legs and under their arms. Call "Time." Ask the observers to tell what they saw.

Ask the child to tell what he felt. Ask those in the circle to tell what they felt.[7] The children may express anger or puzzlement.

Ask, *Who in Bible times wanted to get into the "circle"—to be loved and accepted as part of a group, not to feel left out? Today we are going to talk about some people who felt left out.*

To what kind of place do the words golden goblets, couches, splendor, and court take you? Look up Esther 2:7 and 15 in your Bibles. What words does the writer use to describe Esther? How would you feel if someone told you that you had to move to another town? Another house? Look up Esther 7:5 and 6. In what ways does the writer make the reader aware of Esther's anger? Did she have reason to be angry? Do you ever have reason to be angry? What words does she use to describe Haman in verse 6? Are those "praising" words?

Help the children develop a concept of Haman as a selfish, inconsiderate person. Ask, *How are you feeling towards Haman? Is there anything about this story that makes you smile? Would you call Esther a hero?*

Ask, *How could a group as small as ours make any difference in a world in which there is so much prejudice? Have you ever shut anyone out of the "circle" or made someone feel left out of a group? How can you say "I'm sorry?"*

ANGER

(Genesis 25:29-34)

RESOURCES

"bow" (no arrow)
"cooking fire"
beard material
bowls
chalk
chalk/markerboard
felt tip pens
ingredients for lentil stew (see recipe)
paper
rug
"slingshot"
sticks
"stirrer"
"stones"
unleavened bread (ex.: tortillas)

Lentil Stew

7 c. chicken broth
2 chicken bouillon cubes dissolved in 1 c. boiling water
½ lb. dry lentils
1 onion, chopped
⅓ bunch celery, chopped
½ c. parsley, chopped
8 oz. can stewed tomatoes
¾ c. small egg noodles, broken/uncooked
⅛ c. long grain rice, uncooked
Pepper

In a crockpot, combine chicken broth, lentils, onion, celery, and tomatoes. Simmer 4 hours. Add noodles, parsley, and rice. Cook 30 minutes longer. Serves 8.

PREPARATION

> Read Genesis 25:29-34.

> Make lentil stew.

> If possible, arrange to hold class outside.

> Set up a campfire made of stones or sticks.

> Place a rug and bowl beside the fire.

> Put another bowl on the fire with a stirrer in it to look like something is cooking.

PROCEDURE

Dress a child in biblical costume who will stir the food. Dress another child as Esau, with bow (no arrows) and slingshot. Use some beard material (see p. 31) for his hairy arms and beard. Position him some distance away.

Seat children in a semicircle. Tell the story of Jacob and Esau and the loss of the birthright.

Point out Esau and observe his appearance. Ask, *How does the writer appeal to our senses in Genesis 25:29-34? Which of our senses does the story appeal to?* List responses on a chalk/markerboard or paper. Say, *Can't you just smell the stew cooking? Genesis 25:34 in the New Revised Standard Version of the Bible tells us that the stew Esau wanted from Jacob was lentil stew. Lentils are mentioned several times in the Bible as one of the foods people ate. They were small peas. Let's look up 2 Samuel 17:28 and Ezekiel 4:9.*

Serve lentil stew and bread. Ask the children to dip the bread into the stew.

Say, *Jacob and Esau did not have a very happy home. Jacob was the favorite son of his mother, and Esau was the favorite son of his father. Do you understand that all families have problems? What was the biggest problem in the home of Isaac and Rebekah?* (Probably favoritism and jealousy)

Ask, *When you grow up, what will you remember about your childhood home? Could it be your mom's cooking? Can you remember how it smelled and tasted? Will you remember running out to meet your dad when he came in from work? Will you have memories of playing outside in puddles when it rained, or catching lightning bugs on a dark night? Will you think about what your house looked like outside, or the happiness inside—or maybe the unhappiness? Will you see a picture in your mind of going barefoot, how much the*

42

rocks hurt your feet, or walking in the grass, wet with dew, early in the morning?

Say, *One of the men in our story today had memories of his home as a child, but he was afraid to go back there. That's because after the story of the two men and the stew and the selling of the birthright, Jacob deceived his father by pretending to be Esau, in order to get the blessing meant for Esau. To make matters worse, his mother helped him trick his father. It didn't work out so well because Esau found out about it and was very angry. Jacob had to flee the country, and then he and his mother were separated for a long time. Would you say that trickery is a good thing? That's why Jacob was afraid to go home.*

Ask, *What does this story tell you about the kind of person Rebekah was? Who was the angry person in the story? In what ways does Esau remind you of yourself sometimes? Have you ever felt the way he did? Which character reminds you most of yourself? Which one do you like the most? Does this mean you could change some things about yourself for the better? What do you suppose gave Jacob the idea to deceive his father? If the father in a family was away, the older son was in charge, and the family had to obey him. What kind of family leader do you think Esau was? Remember that Jesus was also the oldest child in his family.*

Sing a song about Jacob (see p. 175). Ask the children to help you think of a short, descriptive title for this story of Jacob and Esau. Ask them to complete the worksheet "Think About It" (see p. 45).

Thinking Activites

PROCEDURE

Use the Think Stop (see p. 11) for some of the following tasks to help children see certain Bible stories with more perceptive eyes. Ask the following questions,

- How is the language in this Bible passage different from the language you and I use? For instance, what would a daughter-in-law today say in place of, "Do not press me to leave you, or to turn back from following you?"

- What other ending would you like to give the story if you could?

- Which lines make the story funny? Which lines make it sad? If it were a play and you used music with it, would the music be sad, happy, or bouncy?

- Try to picture the scene of the people crying over _____'s death. Tell me some things you see.

- What words did the writer use to tell us how bright the fire was?

- Which is true in the story? Which is imaginary?

- Put yourself in _____'s place. Imagine her thoughts.

- Does _____ seem like an ordinary person to you? This story tells us a lot about him but not everything. What else would you like to know?

- What are some of the good times _____ and _____ had together?

- How would the grass feel? Cold? Wet? Scratchy?

- Which sentence sums up all the ideas of the story?

- How were those days exciting? Would you like to have lived then? Do exciting things still happen?

- Which character changed the most in the story?

PONDERING

43

- Look for vivid word pictures, for example, the lapping water and the dipping oars. Sketch them on paper.

- Point out the difference between fact and opinion. Which is which?

- Note _____'s character-revealing thoughts and acts.

- Tell which of _____'s ways you think people wondered about.

- Evaluate the difficult decision _____ had to make and the facts that influenced him in making it.

- Tell what qualities _____ had that you did not know she possessed.

- Speculate on how much time was covered in the story. What words make you aware of the passing of time?

- Make a character analysis of each person. Find clues to the characters' thoughts, feelings, reactions, fears, and joys.

- Tell which conversation in the story the writer uses to show us _____'s character.

- Note the importance of the writer's choice of words.

- Think of one word that best describes _____.

- Express feelings the psalm gives you about mountains and rivers.

- Define a real fear and also a foolish fear or superstition.

- Ponder the value of dreams. What personal qualities can help a person make dreams into reality? Do you have those qualities?

- Tell what kind of day it was—the time, the weather, and so on. How do you know that?

- Read the lines that tell you _____ succeeded in his mission.

- Point out the similarities between _____ and _____.

- Tell how _____ remained in character throughout the end of the story.

- Close your eyes. Try to picture the area around _____.

Creative Activities

Creative writing and art are wonderful mediums for children to express their feelings. Encourage honest expression. Don't analyze what they have written or drawn. Consider using these worksheets at the end of this chapter: "Newsflash," "Finish This," "What If . . .," "Sad Faces," "Let's Pretend," "Ruth and Naomi," "Joseph," "My Feelings."

Notes

[1] Rosemary Carr and Stephen Vincent Benet, "Nancy Hanks, 1784–1818"; and Julius Silberger, "A Reply to Nancy Hanks," in *Time for Poetry*, May Hill Arbuthnot, ed. (Glenview IL: HarperCollins, 1961) 40.

[2] Adapted from *Faith for Life Curriculum* (Pittsburgh: Logos System Assoc., 1989).

[3] Ridgeway Addison, *An Activity for Children* (Kirkwood MO: Kirkwood Baptist Church). Used by permission.

[4] Ibid. Adapted from Fred H. Wight, *Manners and Customs of Bible Lands* (Chicago: Moody Press, 1953) 113.

[5] Adapted from Peter Farb, *The Land, Wildlife, and Peoples of the Bible* (New York: Harper & Row, 1967) 81.

[6] Ibid., 5.

[7] Adapted from Bruce Joyce and Marsha Weil, *Models of Teaching* (Needham MA: Allyn & Bacon, 1986) 184-85.

PONDERING

Think about It!

Sometimes it is helpful to express on paper what we feel. It helps to get some hurtful (or happy) feelings on the outside instead of keeping them on the inside. Answer the following questions honestly. No one will see this sheet!

What at home bothers you more than anything else?

What would you change if you could?

What are the 5 "don'ts" you hear most often from your parents?

(1)

(2)

(3)

(4)

(5)

With whom do you get along best in your family? Why?

With whom can you not get along in the family? Why?

What are some things you could change about yourself that would help everyone in your family have a happier home?

Choose one person in your family. Write down not only what that person looks like, but what he or she is like inside.

Newsflash

Name a Bible character.

List 4 words or phrases that describe this person.

-

-

-

-

Pretend you are the anchorperson on a TV news program. You have been asked to write a 2-minute news brief about the person named above. Use the space below to write your news brief. (You will be given the scripture reference to read for your preparation.)

_____

_____

_____

_____

_____

_____

_____

_____

_____

_____

Finish This

Draw cartoons and write captions that express your feelings about the situations below.

What If . . .?

Look at a Bible story picture. Write about how your life would be different if you were a person in the picture.

_____

_____

_____

_____

_____

_____

Sad Faces

What makes you more jealous than anything? Think back to a time when you were jealous of someone or wanted something someone else had. How did you feel? Write about it below. Don't let anyone see your paper. It's yours to take home.

_____

_____

_____

_____

_____

Let's Pretend . . .

Pretend you are Miriam, Moses' sister. Your brother is 3 months old, and the Pharaoh wants to kill him. Your mother made a basket for him and put him in the Nile River. Now she has told you to watch him and see what happens. You know that Pharaoh's daughter will come to bathe in the river. Use the space below to express how scared you are.

_____

_____

_____

_____

_____

_____

_____

Joseph

Pretend you are Joseph. You were thrown in a pit to die and then sold into slavery. Some traders came by, treated you roughly, and then carried you away to Egypt. Now you are in a strange land far away from your family. You are 17 years old. Write below how you feel and what you are thinking.

_____

_____

_____

_____

_____

_____

_____

Ruth and Naomi

Using the words below and the space provided, write a story about Ruth and Naomi (see Ruth 1, 2).

alone
barley
Bethlehem
Boaz
harvest workers
Judah
Moab
Orpah
your people
25 pounds

My Feelings

Write a word in the blank that expresses your true feelings about the situation named.

I felt _____ when I got an "A" on a test.

I felt _____ when my Dad scolded me.

I felt _____ when my (pet, grandmother, grandfather, uncle, aunt, etc.) died.

I feel _____ when my parents start talking about earthquakes.

I feel _____ when I'm around my best friend.

I feel _____ when I hear about war.

I feel _____ when I see snow falling.

I feel _____ when my parents are nicer to my sister/brother than they are to me.

I feel _____ when I am in a warm shower.

I feel _____ when my stomach is growling from hunger and I finally get something to eat.

I feel _____ when my parents go on a trip and I'm left behind.

I feel _____ when I think about God.

Chapter 6
NARRATING: Telling Stories to Encourage Feedback

Rationale

Storytelling is probably the oldest method of teaching. For centuries good stories have fascinated people. In biblical times people used the stories of their ancestors to hold on to their faith in perilous times. Stories were handed down from generation to generation.

What stories do you remember from your own childhood? What helps you remember them? As adults, we may quickly apply stories to our own lives and base our behavior on lessons learned from those stories. Application of the facts doesn't come so easily for children, however. They need immediate feedback to reinforce the events of a story in their minds.

When telling stories . . .

- Know the needs of your audience.
- Know the story well.(Study the characters; put yourself in their place. What would they smell, touch, see, hear?
- Decide what facts and feelings you wish to convey.
- Remove jewelry or any other distraction.
- Sit on the children's level.
- Maintain good eye contact.
- Don't just read the story aloud from any source.
- Use a quiet voice; children will listen more closely.
- Present an attention-getting introduction.
- Leave out unnecessary details.
- Be dynamic; show expression.
- Finish the story in one session.
- Answer questions.
- Seek immediate feedback by using games, music, question-and-answer review, pictures, etc.

The stories and activities in this chapter are given for examples. You can easily adapt the ideas to other stories.

Jesus, the Leader
(Mark 6:1-6; Luke 4:16-30; Matthew 13:54-58)

RESOURCES
chalk/markerboard or paper
chalk or felt tip pens
picture of Jesus speaking to a crowd

PREPARATION
> Print the following on chalk/markerboard or paper:

Nazareth	Yes
Capernaum	Yes
Tiberius	Yes
Jerusalem	No
Bethsaida	Yes
Beersheba	No
Jericho	No

PROCEDURE
Tell the following story:

The people of Jesus' hometown didn't want to hear what he had to say. In fact, they were angry with him. "Who does he think he is, claiming to be 'God's Son'?" they demanded. "We watched him grow up. He's just a carpenter."

On one occasion, Jesus really irritated them. He went to the synagogue on the Sabbath. He was invited to read the scripture. He read from the book of Isaiah. He told the people that the verses described him. "How important he thinks he is!" the people were thinking. They became so angry that they took him to a nearby cliff and were going to throw him off, but Jesus just disappeared through the crowd. In spite of their disapproval, he kept on teaching and preaching to many people.

Does anyone here know what a levee is? You would know if you had lived in Missouri during the "great flood of '93." As more and more levees broke, water from rivers and streams poured into farmland and towns. What are bayous? You would know if you lived in the state of Louisiana.

You and I often talk about things other people don't understand. Jesus didn't do that. As he was growing up, his mind recorded pictures of life all around him: a hen and her chicks, weddings, funerals, honest and dishonest people, farmers planting seeds, shepherds and sheep, filling oil lamps, selling grain in the marketplace, a yoke of oxen, . . . He later used these familiar things to tell wonderful stories. He got people's attention by talking about things they understood.

Jesus often taught great crowds of people. How did the crowds hear him with all the noise? Do you think the people were so spellbound by what he said that they sat very still and listened well? Jesus was a wonderful storyteller.

Say, *We're going to play a game called "What Is Important About the 'Yesses'?"* After some direction, the children may discover that the "yesses" are all towns in Galilee, places where Jesus did most of his teaching. In fact, for a time, Capernaum was his headquarters. It was a busy port with fishermen, boats, fish markets, and a synagogue.[1]

Say, *Let's think for a moment about some of the big crowds Jesus taught. Can you think of some of those large groups?* They may suggest the feeding of the 5,000 and the crowd listening to the Sermon on the Mount.

Show a picture of Jesus speaking to a large crowd. Ask, *Do you think this was a typical crowd we might see in our time? Help me picture the scene. Name some people who were probably there.*

List responses on chalk/markerboard or paper. They may say older people, bent and stooped and who didn't hear well; people talking and moving about; crying children; teenagers in love.

Ask, *Where did Jesus do most of his teaching, and to whom? What did he talk about? Were there people who never believed he was the Son of God?*

Instructions from God
(Genesis 12, 17, 18)

RESOURCES
4 upright sticks
Bible
black fabric
bread
cheese
compass
construction paper (black and brown)
costume
"goatskin water bag"
I.D. card
razor
sandals
"shepherd's staff"
suitcase
suntan lotion
"tent"
toothbrush

PREPARATION

> If you meet outdoors, set up a small tent by securing 4 upright sticks in the ground at 4 corners and placing black fabric over them. If you meet inside, place black fabric over a table or a few chairs.

> Pack a suitcase with the following items: a toothbrush, a razor, a replica of a goatskin water bag (see p. 14) cut out of black construction paper, an extra Bible costume, cheese and bread, a shepherd's staff cut out of brown construction paper, an I.D. card, a compass, sandals, suntan lotion, and a Bible.

PROCEDURE

Tell the story of Abraham:

Abram was called by God and told to take his family, flocks, and herds and go to a land God would show him. The caravan started on the long trip. Herdsmen drove the flocks of animals. At night the women set up black tents of goats' hair, placing pegs in the ground to hold them. God promised Abram that if he would obey God, he would "become the father of a great nation" and his descendants would be more than the stars of the sky.

One day Abram heard God's voice telling him that his name would no longer be Abram, meaning "exalted father." His name would be Abraham, or "father of a nation." As Abraham sat in front of the tent, he saw 3 strangers approaching slowly. They told Abraham that he and his wife Sarah would be the parents of a son. The story of the strangers was hard to believe because Abraham and Sarah were old, but Abraham knew that God keeps His promises. Eventually, Sarah gave birth to a son. The proud parents named him Isaac. God kept His promise.

Take the objects out of the suitcase one at a time, and ask, *Which of these would Abram take on his trip? What else would he take that isn't in this bag?*

Talk about the problems of putting together a caravan. Ask if it would be something like organizing a parade. Ask the children if they would like to make a long trip with a caravan.

The Generous Hostess

(Acts 16:11-15)

RESOURCES

clothes rack or chairs
large pieces of purple fabric
masking tape
strips of paper

PREPARATION

> Display large pieces of fabric in various shades of purple. You might drape them over a portable clothes drying rack or over several chairs.

> Print the following questions on strips of paper. Tape them underneath chairs, ladders, beanbag chairs, tables, and so forth. The answers are given for the leader.

- In what city did Lydia live? (Thyatira) (Acts 16:14)
- Lydia was a businesswoman. What did she sell? Why was it so expensive? (purple cloth) (Acts 16:14) (It was dyed with the juice of the best shellfish on the beaches of the Mediterranean shores.[2] It was hard work to dye it.)
- Who were the three missionaries who came to town? (Paul, Silas, and Timothy) (Acts 15:40; 16:1-3)
- To what town did the missionaries come? (Philippi) (Acts 16:11-13)
- Where in Philippi did Lydia meet the three missionaries? (by the river at a place of prayer) (Acts 16:13, 14)
- What group of people had gathered at the river prayer meeting? (women) (Acts 16:13)
- Was Lydia a Christian before she met Paul, Silas, and Timothy? (No, but she worshiped God) (Acts 16:14-15)
- What good thing did Lydia do for the missionaries? (invited them to stay at her house) (Acts 16:15)

PROCEDURE

Tell the story:

Lydia lived in the city of Thyatira. Her business was selling purple cloth. She had come to Philippi to worship God. She and other women were having a prayer meeting down by the river. One day 3 missionaries came to the river prayer meeting and preached about Jesus. They were Paul, Silas, and Timothy. Lydia had believed in God for some time, but she didn't know about Jesus. The missionaries taught her about Jesus. Lydia believed in him and was baptized. She was so happy she invited the missionaries to stay at her house.

NARRATING

Ask the children to find the hidden questions and answer them. Then ask them to write a short statement showing the difference between being a believer in God only and being a believer in Jesus.

The Man with a Message

(Matthew 3:1-6)

RESOURCES
beard material
"camel's hair" clothing
carob chocolate
dried locusts
"girdle"
honey
paper
pencils
sandals

PREPARATION

> Purchase food samples (perhaps from a health food store) such as John the Baptist would have eaten: dried locusts, honey, and chocolate made from the carob tree.

PROCEDURE

Dress a child as John the Baptist. Include a tunic that resembles camel's hair clothing, a "leather" girdle (belt) around his waist, sandals, a beard, and unkempt hair. Position John behind the children in an inconspicuous place.

Introduce the story:

Can you name any of the desert areas in the United States? There were 3 desert areas in Palestine: the Negeb, the Sinai, and the wilderness of Judea. The people of Israel today have learned how to make the bare deserts produce again. The Negeb desert was very dry until recently when archaeologists found the wells that had not supplied water for thousands of years since Isaac. Now those same wells supply water for Israeli communities. Can you believe that?

John the Baptist lived in one of the desert areas of Palestine—the wilderness of Judea. Who was this man? Why was he so important? Give the children a few minutes to answer. *Some people think he was one of the Essenes who lived near the Dead Sea in a place called Qumran. The Essenes stayed to themselves, translated scriptures, and then hid them for safekeeping. In 1947, a Bedouin shepherd boy found some scrolls hidden in pottery jars. They are called the Dead Sea Scrolls. Some Bible scholars believe the scrolls may have been put there by the Essenes.*

John spent his time preaching and baptizing people. Pause to allow John to say in a loud, booming voice from the back of the room: "Turn away from your sins because the Kingdom of Heaven is near." *He even had his own disciples. Later many of his followers became disciples of Jesus. John was a relative of Jesus. Do you know how they were related? One day Jesus went to the Jordan River where John was baptizing and asked to be baptized. John said, "Instead, I should be baptized by you." But Jesus insisted. Jesus set an example for us. It was also the beginning of his great work in helping people.*

Ask John to come forward from the back of the room. Ask the children to describe on paper how he looks.

Read Matthew 3:4. Say, *Some people who study the Bible believe that the locusts mentioned in verse 4 were actually grasshoppers. Other people believe they were not grasshoppers at all but pods from the carob, or locust, tree that were fed to farm animals. When ripe, the pods have a dark, honeylike syrup. For this reason, the carob tree is sometimes called the "St. John's Bread Tree."*[5] Encourage the children to taste dried locusts, honey, and chocolate made from carob.

The Wasteful Son

(Luke 15:11-32)

RESOURCES

backdrop of biblical times farm
Bible for each child
costume
dirty, ragged clothing
picture of the prodigal son

PREPARATION

> Ask several children to paint on table paper a simple backdrop for the story. Include a biblical house in the distance, a winding road, and farm animals of that time. Or, arrange to take the children to a working farm where they can have a picnic and see animals and a pigpen.

> Find a picture depicting the story of the prodigal son.

PROCEDURE

Dress a child as the prodigal son in torn, dirty, ragged clothing and bare feet. Ask him to sit beside the leader with his head in his hands, looking forlorn. Dress another child in Bible costume. Ask her to stand in a corner with her back to the group.

Say, *Our story isn't just a story about a boy leaving home. You can help me tell the story by finding Luke 15 in your Bibles and answering the questions I'll ask.*

Read verses 11-12. Why do you think the father didn't say "No" when the younger son asked for his share of the property?

Look at verse 16. After the younger son left home, he became so poor that he "would gladly have filled himself with the pods that the pigs were eating." These were pods from the carob tree, which were fed to farm animals. The beans that grow in the pods somewhat resemble our green peas. Today, in the Near East, the pods provide fodder for animals and food for very poor people. In Jesus'

time people did not eat the pods unless they were as hungry as the wasteful son.[4]

Read verses 13 and 14. Why do you think the boy is called the "wasteful son?"

Read verse 17. What is the meaning of "when he came to himself?"

Read verse 21. Did the son come home because he realized how much he was hurting his family, or because he was tired, dirty, and hungry? Is being tired, dirty, and hungry enough reason to come home and say, "I'm sorry?"

Read verse 23. What is so special about the "fatted calf"? See p. 167.

Ask the children what they have learned from this story. Give them time to discuss their answers.

Ask the younger son to exit. Ask the older brother to enter. Ask him the following questions: *How did you feel when you saw the party your father was giving for your brother? What if you were your brother? Would you feel differently about the welcome-home party? Maybe your father just wanted to see him. It had been a long time. You don't seem too angry now. When did you begin to get over your anger?*

Ask the children, *What is the danger in getting extremely angry? What can you do before you get to that point?* They may say: walk away, take a breather, or think about the consequences. Turn to the older son. Ask, *Did you do any of those things?* Turn to the other children in the room. Ask, *Can you sense how the older brother felt? Do you blame him? If not, is there any value in doing the right thing and trying to please God?*

NARRATING

Question the children about where the mother was in this story. Did the "wasteful son" have sisters who grieved for him also? Say, **No one knows if this story is true. It's called a parable. What is a parable?** Make sure the children understand that a parable is a story, either true or imaginary, that teaches a truth.

A Mighty Warrior
(Judges 6, 7, 8)

RESOURCES
locusts
raw sweet potatoes
recording of a Marian Anderson song
"sheaves of wheat"

PREPARATION
> Research the stories of George Washington Carver and Marian Anderson.

> Review "The Harvesting of Grain" (see p. 15) as background for telling the story.

> Purchase some locusts from a bait and tackle shop. Take them to class for the children to see.

> Place sheaves of wheat (see p. 13) where you will tell the story.

> Cut slices of raw sweet potatoes.

PROCEDURE
Ask the children to define the word "warrior."

Tell the following story:

The threshing, or beating out, of grain was an interesting necessity in biblical times. A threshing floor was an important place. There was a time when Gideon could go to the threshing floor or openly thresh grain outside, and work without being afraid. But now there were desert raiders who attacked his flocks and herds, burned and looted, and left Gideon and his family with nothing to eat.

One day an angel appeared to Gideon, who was secretly threshing wheat in a wine press because of his fear of his enemies. The angel said, "The Lord is with you, you mighty warrior." Gideon was a humble man, and so he doubted that compliment. But then, when God chooses great leaders, they usually don't think they're so great. But the angel told Gideon just what to do. Gideon gave a mighty blast on a ram's horn and summoned an army. To his surprise, he was informed that his army was too big! Look in Judges 7:4-8 to find out how God told him to reduce his army. Soldiers who lapped water like dogs remained in the army; those who knelt to drink were eliminated from the army.

Gideon looked out on the tents of his enemies. The tents looked as thick as grasshoppers. It was a scary sight. Exodus 10:14 and 15 says that in Egypt during Moses' time, "they (the grasshoppers/locusts/crickets) came in swarms and settled over the whole country. . . . They covered the ground until it was black with them." Show the locusts to the children. *In recent years one black cloud of the insects, which blotted out the sun, was estimated to be 1 mile wide and more than 50 miles from front to back. Imagine how Gideon felt as he looked at all those tents. Nevertheless, Gideon knew that God was with him.*

Ask another leader in the room to read aloud Judges 7:16-22 to find out how Gideon defeated the army of the Midianites. Ask the children to follow along in their Bibles. Conclude the story:

And that's how God called a man from threshing wheat to become a mighty soldier!

Ask, **Does this story remind you of any other Bible stories about victory over an enemy? Name them. Can you name people in past years of world history whom God has called from seemingly unimportant jobs to become great leaders? Do you know the stories of**

George Washington Carver and Marian Anderson? Share information about Carver and Anderson. Play the Anderson recording. Distribute samples of raw sweet potatoes. Tell the children how Carver discovered 118 uses of the sweet potato, such as using it to make potato flour, shoepolish, and candy.

Joshua, Faithful Leader

(Joshua 6:1-20)

RESOURCES
boxes or blocks of different sizes

PREPARATION

> Move equipment away from the center of the room.

> Stack several boxes or blocks of different sizes on top of each other.

PROCEDURE
Ask a child to look up Ezekiel 4:2 and be prepared to read it to the group. Station a child on top of a 4' stepladder. Introduce him as the guard on top of the city wall. He peers into the distance.

Tell the story:

Joshua knew that Moses was going to die and that he was the man chosen by God to take Moses' place. But he also knew that he had to conquer enemy cities and overrun them in order for the Israelites to enter Caanan. It was a scary job!

One of the cities Joshua and his soldiers were to overtake was Jericho, an old, walled city. It was frightening even getting near the wall. During attacks, soldiers on top of the wall threw spears, stones, and blazing torches at their enemies, and poured hot oil down on them. They also used bows and arrows, and their aim was good. The city walls were so thick, the approaching army often used

catapults and battering rams. A catapult was a machine used to throw stones. A battering ram was a large machine with a sharp, arrow-like device that jutted out from the front. Soldiers built a mound made of stone and other materials that reached up to the city wall. Then men rolled the battering ram into the wall until they knocked it down and captured their enemies inside.[5] Ask the child who looked up Ezekiel 4:2 to read it now. *God had a better plan for Joshua.*

The people of Jericho were like prisoners inside the city walls, too scared to come out because of Joshua and his men. And then God gave instructions to Joshua for how to take over the city. God said, "You and your men shall march around the city once each day for 7 days. The Ark of the Covenant is to go ahead of the marchers, and 7 priests are to blow 7 trumpets of rams' horns. On the 7th day, you are to march around the city 7 times. As soon as you hear the priests make 1 long blast on the trumpets, then all the people outside the wall are to shout with a great shout, and the city will fall down. Then you and your men can take over the people inside." Joshua gave these instructions to his followers, and they did exactly as God told them to do. On the 7th day, the walls of Jericho fell, and Joshua and his men were able to take over the city. It was a great victory.

Begin a "talk fest" about what you just read. Discuss the possibilities of the Israelites winning the battle if God had not helped them.

Ask the children to sit in a circle around the boxes, which represent the walls of Jericho. Ask the following questions based on Joshua 6:1-24. Answers are given for the leader. When the children have correctly answered 7 questions, they may "tear down" Jericho.[6]

- Was anyone going in or out of the city of Jericho? Why or why not? (no) (v. 1)
- How many times were the people to circle the city for the first 6 days? (once) (v. 3)
- Describe the trumpets. (They were ram's horns) (v. 4)
- Who was to blow the trumpets? (the priests) (v. 4)
- What is the "ark" in this passage? (Ark of the Covenant)
- On the 7th day, what were the people to do as soon as the trumpets were blown? (shout with a loud shout) (v. 16)
- Was God's plan successful? (yes)
- What were the people not to keep for themselves? (silver and gold, bronze and iron vessels) (vv. 18, 19)
- Who was the woman who, along with her family, was saved from being killed? (Rahab) (v. 23)
- What happened to the city of Jericho when the Israelites got inside? (Joshua and his soldiers burned it.) (v. 24)
- Would you like to have been there? Why or why not?

Building the Tabernacle

(Exodus 35:4–40:33)

RESOURCES

Bible for each child
black fabric
blocks of wood (2)
cans of soda pop
chalk or felt tip pens
chalk/markerboard or paper
coins
hammers (2)
jewelry (gold, silver, with stones)
leather belt
map of Bible lands
oil in a bottle
paper cup for each child
picture of people bringing gifts to the tabernacle
picture of the tabernacle
small table
spice
wooden blocks (2)
yarn (blue, purple, red)

PREPARATION

> Move all room equipment to the wall.

> Display one small table, covered with black fabric to represent the goats' hair tabernacle.

> Display teaching pictures.

PROCEDURE

Send a child to the Searching Stop to look up the word "tabernacle." Ask the children to sit on the floor around the tabernacle. Distribute the following items: gold and silver jewelry; blue, purple, and red yarn; a leather belt; oil in a bottle; some kind of spice; and some jewelry with stones in it. Ask the children to stand and hold up these items as you talk about each gift for the tabernacle, and then to bring them to the storyteller, who will display them.

Have someone make the sound of hammers hitting wood. Say, *God gave a covenant, or promise, to Moses on Mount Sinai. What was it called? God wanted the people to know that God was living among them. God wanted them to have a special place of worship. God gave Moses a very special plan for building the worship center and also told Moses exactly what to put inside the building. The people were to bring gifts for the building.* Ask the children to look up Exodus 25:1-9 in their Bibles and to name the gifts the people were to bring. List responses on paper or a chalk/markerboard.

Say, *The tabernacle was dedicated to God on the 1st day of the 2nd year after the Israelites left Egypt. Up until then in Jewish history, people had worshiped God only at altars; they had no buildings for worship. So you might call the tabernacle the first "church."* Ask the assigned child to define tabernacle.

Say, *There were no trees to shade the tabernacle. It must have been hot inside. There were 2 rooms in the tabernacle divided by a veil. Only the high priest went into the smaller of the 2* rooms called the Holy of Holies, and that only once a year on the Day of Atonement. The tabernacle stood in the center of the camp where the Israelites lived. The tents of the people formed an outer circle around it. Why did God want this building to be a tent? How long do you suppose it took the people to pack it up when they got ready to move to another place?

The people offered sacrifices for their sins at the Altar of Burnt Offering in the courtyard. Do you want to know something amazing about this story? Priest Aaron put a lamb on the altar as a sacrifice for the sins of the people. He did not put any fire on the altar, but God sent fire to burn up the sacrifice. From that time on, every morning and evening, a sacrifice was offered, and the fire that God had started was never allowed to go out. Even when the tabernacle moved, the priests carried burning coals from the altar in a covered pan on the trip. The tabernacle was very important in the worship of God.

Say, *The people had very few things with them in the wilderness. Where did the gifts they gave for the tabernacle come from? Find the answer in Exodus 12:31-36.*

On the map point out Egypt and the tabernacle.

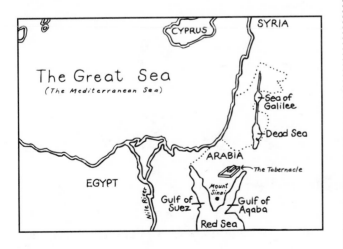

Say, *The tabernacle was placed in a courtyard that measured 150 cubits. If a cubit equals approximately 18", how big was the courtyard in feet? There were beautiful drapes made of linen, an altar on which to offer sacrifices to God, and the laver in which the priests washed their hands and feet. The tabernacle itself was a tent building that measured 30x10 cubits. The finest goats' hair was used to cover it. Again, do some math. How many inches are in a cubit? Figure the dimensions of the tabernacle. The framework from the ground up was 10 cubits. How high was it in feet?* If you have a large open area, you may want to send several children outside to measure it in the grass. Then take the rest of the group out to see how big it was. To what building does it compare in size?

Talk with the children about cooperation. Ask in what ways cooperation was needed to build the tabernacle. To illustrate cooperation, collect change from the children. Buy cans of soda pop with the money. Give each child a paper cup. Divide the soda. There probably will be complaints for the small amounts given. State that when people do not give much, there is very little that can be used. This is why God asked the people to give generously for the tabernacle.

A Job for Jeremiah

(Jeremiah 35–38)

RESOURCES

Bibles
black pen or sharpened dowel stick dipped in black ink
cassette player
cassette tape
Hebrew letter samples
old shirts
paper
picture of Jeremiah

PREPARATION

> Display a large picture of Jeremiah.

> Record the following story on cassette tape:

NARRATING

Jeremiah was a prophet. He tried to convince the people of his country to be faithful to God and God's laws. But the people did not listen. They continued to do things their way. Jeremiah even went to Jerusalem, but the angry people there asked King Jehoiakim to keep Jeremiah away from the Temple. God knew that Jeremiah was sad, so God said, "Write my words on a scroll." Jeremiah asked Baruch, a scribe, to write the words Jeremiah told him. It was a long, hard job.

Baruch went to the Temple and read the words. But the officials in the king's palace advised Baruch and Jeremiah to hide from the king for their own safety. Then the officials gave the scroll to the king. He was so angry that, as the scroll was read to him, he cut it into pieces and burned it in the fire. Then God told Jeremiah to take another scroll and again to dictate the message to Baruch.

In the meantime, a new king began to rule. His name was Zedekiah. Some of Jeremiah's enemies went to King Zedekiah. They said, "Jeremiah is discouraging us. He should be put to death." So Jeremiah was put into a cistern, a tank to collect rainwater. There was no water in the cistern, only mud, and Jeremiah sank in it. But Ebed-melech, a helper in the king's house, told the king that Jeremiah would die if he were not rescued. So the king sent 3 men to take Jeremiah out of the well. Jeremiah cleaned himself up and went to live in the court of the guard. Then King Zedekiah promised Jeremiah that he would never put him to death nor turn him over to the men who wanted him dead.

Baruch had a difficult but important job as a scribe. Scribes recorded much of the information we read in our Bibles. A scribe could be recognized by the pen case or inkhorn hanging from his belt. His equipment included reed pens, an ink well, and a small knife for erasing and cutting the papyrus. Papyrus was a plant that grew in the marshes, or low, wet ground overgrown with grass. It was sliced, pressed, and allowed to dry so that it could be written on. The ink had to be black.[7]

Scribes also wrote on parchment, a material made from animal skins. The same writing equipment was used by young boys in the synagogue school.[8]

Ink well

Often scribes scratched their letters into clay while it was soft. Then it was baked to make it hard. In later times, a piece of wood or ivory was carved out. Melted wax was poured inside. When it cooled, it became hard and easy to scratch letters on. Each writer used a pen called a "stylus" to write in the wax.[9]

PROCEDURE

Play the taped story.

Give each child a piece of light-colored paper and a black pen or a sharpened dowel stick dipped in black ink. Cover each child's clothing with an old shirt. Ask the children to start copying Matthew 23:1-4. If they become discouraged, ask, **At that rate, how long would it have taken Baruch to copy Jeremiah's words? Count the number of words in Jeremiah 36:4, 32.** Ask the children also to copy some Hebrew letters, beginning on the right side of the paper and moving to the left.

Hebrew letters

Help the children understand how discouraged Baruch and Jeremiah were when their work was destroyed.

Notes

[1]Teaching method adapted from Bruce Joyce and Marsha Weil, *Models of Teaching* (Needham MA: Allyn & Bacon, 1986) 25-26.

[2]Adapted from Chris Tarrant, *Life in Bible Times* (Nashville: Scripture Union, 1985) 38. Used by permission.

[3]Adapted from Peter Farb, *The Land, Wildlife, and Peoples of the Bible* (New York: Harper & Row, 1967) 137-38.

[4]Ibid., 138.

[5]Adapted from Tarrant, 28-29.

[6]Adapted from Mary Lois Sanders and Audra Tull, "Learning from Joshua," *Formations*, Year 2, Trimester 2 (Macon GA: Smyth & Helwys Publishing, Inc.) 39.

[7]Adapted from *Marketplace, 29 A.D.: A Bible Times Experience* (Stevensville MI: B. J. Goetz Publishing Co., 1989) 109-110.

[8]Adapted from *Jesus and His Times* (Pleasantville NY: Reader's Digest Assoc., 1987) 158.

[9]Adapted from Marion C. Armstrong, *How the Bible Came to Us* (Nashville: Abingdon Press, 1943) 3.

Chapter 7
MOLDING: Developing Values and Ethics

Rationale

Making choices is a basic need of children. Children are looking for models, trying to understand their own roles and also life choices. They are developing a conscience, morality, and a sense of values that will last a lifetime. They choose to have either great respect, some respect, or no respect for moral rules and laws. They are influenced by examples that are attractive to them, moral teachings in the Bible, values of their own peer group, approval or disapproval by adults, and the freedom (or lack of freedom) to make their own decisions.

Children develop numerous opinions, mental impressions, and ideas based on their everyday experiences. They are exposed to many types of people who influence their lives. They can think for themselves if given the opportunity to make decisions. They should be offered many problem-solving opportunities. As they solve their own problems, they are forming character. In this chapter I describe activities that can help children see the results of good and bad choices. They should be able to identify with the character traits discussed.[1]

Positive Traits

To help children develop good character, parents and leaders must set boundaries. Children need boundaries, both personally and in the groups of which they are a part. Without limits, children are insecure and uncertain as to what is right or wrong. Explain to the children why parents and leaders set boundaries for them. Ask them to name the "don'ts" they hear most often from adults. Ask them why these "don'ts" are really for their own good. Use the following lessons to help the children learn positive character traits from the examples of biblical people.

DEPENDABILITY
(1 Samuel 1, 2)

RESOURCES
6 placards
chalk/markerboard or paper
picture of Hannah praying

PREPARATION
> Make 6 placards spelling de-pend-a-bil-i-ty.

> Display a picture of Hannah praying.

PROCEDURE
Ask for 6 volunteers. Hang a placard around the neck of each child. Ask the children to quickly arrange themselves in order to form a word. If their mad scramble fails to produce a word, help them. Then write the word "dependability" on a chalk/markerboard or large piece of paper.

Present a word-association quiz. Ask the children to respond with whatever comes to their minds first as they look at the word "dependability." List responses on paper or a chalk/marker board. Say, ***See if the words on the list fit the Bible character we're going to talk about now.***

Show a picture of Hannah praying to God for a son. Tell the story:

More than anything else, Hannah wanted a son. Her friends had sons and daughters. In ancient Israel, it was considered a blessing from God to have sons, because females were not highly thought of. It was considered a curse to be barren, or unable to have children. Some people even made fun of Hannah.

Day after day Hannah prayed. One day she was so upset as she prayed in the Temple that the priest Eli thought she was drunk! She sobbed and sobbed. She promised God if He would give her a son, the child would be His for always and would serve Him.

God sent Hannah and her husband, Elkanah, a son. They named the baby Samuel. When Samuel was able to be away from his mother, Hannah took him to the Temple and left him there to serve God with the priest Eli. And then Hannah prayed a beautiful prayer. Look it up in your Bibles in 1 Samuel 2:1-10. Do you think it was hard for Hannah to go away and leave her only son? Children were weaned between the ages of 2 and 5, and it was then that they were dedicated to God. Look in your Bibles at Genesis 21:8. Do you think Hannah cried as she walked home from the Temple that day? Read in 1 Samuel 1:26-28 her words to Eli as she left the child there.

Do you keep promises? Are you dependable even when it's difficult, or do you forget that you made the promise? Hannah kept her promise. She was dependable. Because she was dependable and kept her promise to God, God gave Hannah other sons and daughters. Many years later, someone else prayed Hannah's beautiful prayer when she found out that God was also going to give her a son. It's actually called "Mary's Song of Praise." Find it in Luke 1:46-55. It almost seems as if Mary copied

Hannah's prayer. She must have known the story of Hannah very well.

Recall a promise you made recently. You can tell it to the group or just think about it. Were you dependable? Did it make you feel good inside to keep your promise? Look at the words you gave earlier to define dependability. Do they describe Hannah? Do they describe you?

LOYALTY

(Daniel 1–6)

RESOURCES

beans
Bible for each child
cabbage
cucumbers
lentils
lettuce
onions
picture of an ancient city wall
pitcher filled with water
table

PREPARATION

> Fill a pitcher with water. Place it on a table. Also place on the table some onions, lentils, beans, cucumbers, cabbage, and lettuce.
(H. W. F. Saggs documents these as some of the vegetables the people of Babylon ate.[2])

> Display a picture of an ancient city wall.

PROCEDURE

Give this background to the story: *In about 587 B.C., King Nebuchadnezzar of Babylon conquered Jerusalem and took many of the people away as captives to Babylon. Because the food ran out, many people in Jerusalem starved to death when he surrounded the city.* Show a picture of an ancient city wall. *From behind the city wall, the people of Jerusalem fought the Babylonians with stones, blazing torches, bows and arrows, and even hot boiling oil! But eventually the Babylonians broke through the wall. One of Nebuchadnezzar's captives was a fine, young man named Daniel. The king wanted Daniel to serve in his court. Eventually King Nebuchadnezzar died, and his son Belshazzar took his place as king. After Belshazzar died, Darius became the new king.*

Ask the children to turn in their Bibles to Daniel 1. Lead in directed Bible study by asking the following questions. Answers are given for leaders.

• Read Daniel 1:3, 7. Daniel and his friends were given new names in Babylon. What were they? (Shadrack, Meshach, and Abednego) Who gave them these names? (Ashpenaz, the chief official)

• What is the problem in this story? (Daniel refused to eat the king's rich food because it was against Jewish law.)

• What was Daniel's choice? (He had to choose between pleasing King Nebuchadnezzar and pleasing God.) Point to the display of vegetables and explain that they are probably the same kinds of vegetables Daniel and his three friends ate.

• Read Daniel 3:1. What god did the people of Babylon worship? (They worshiped many gods, but this one—90′ tall and 9′ wide—was their newest.)

• Find in Daniel 3:4-6 what King Nebuchadnezzar said the people were to do about worshiping this idol. (When they heard music, they were to fall down and worship the statue.)

• Shadrach, Meshach, and Abednego defied the king. What does "defied" mean? (disobeyed)

• According to Daniel 3:19-23, what happened to the three men as a result of their disobedience? (put in a fiery furnace)

• Who do you suppose was praying for them all the time they were in the furnace? (Daniel) Why does it help to pray for others?

• Read Daniel 3:26-29. What convinced the king and others that God had protected the three men? (The men's clothing and hair were not burned; there wasn't even the smell of smoke.)

• Later Daniel was thrown into the den of lions. What crime put him there? (He would not pray to King Darius for 30 days as the king commanded.) Read Daniel 6:21-22 to find out how God protected him. (by shutting the mouths of the lions)

Say, *An ancient sport in biblical times was hunting lions. The lions were captured in nets and pits. After lions are fed, they are very lazy and hardly move for several days. But if they are hungry, they will tear their victims apart. No wild animal is talked about as much in the Bible as the lion. Lions are mentioned in 31 of the 66 books of the Bible. Many of them lived in Palestine during Old Testament times, but now they can hardly be found there.*[3]

Daniel kept his loyalty to God even in hard times. What were the wonderful results of his loyalty? Have you ever had to make a choice similar to Daniel's? Did it make you more popular? If it didn't make you more popular, do you think others at least had respect for your decision? Most important of all, did your decision make you feel better about yourself? Then how would you define the word "loyal?"

ASSERTIVENESS
(Genesis 26)

RESOURCES
dry beans

PREPARATION
> Move room equipment against the wall.

PROCEDURE
Use the following activity[4] to teach assertiveness. Give each child a large handful of beans. Ask each child to use the beans to mark off a small space for him/herself to sit in on the floor. Say, *This is your turf. No one else can come into it. Who else do you know who has turfs of which they feel protective?* They may suggest: gang members, countries, homeowners, and so on. *Who in the Bible had turfs?* They may name specific characters. Suggest that almost everyone had their own piece of land, no matter how small.

Tell the following story:

MOLDING

Isaac lived in the valley of Gerar and became very rich. Earlier the Philistines had filled with dirt the wells that Isaac's father, Abraham, had dug a long time ago. The wells were necessary for the people to have water. Isaac dug Abraham's wells again, but the herdsmen of Gerar said, "This water is ours." Isaac did not fight with them but moved on and dug another well. They quarreled about that well also. Again Isaac did not fight, but he and his servants moved on to Beersheba and dug another well. One day his enemies said, "We won't bother you again; we want to be friends."

Ask, *Do you think Isaac handled the situation well? Was he a coward, or just a man trying to please God by being kind? How do you feel now about your turf, your space inside the beans? If the person sitting next to you wants to take your space, will you give it to him and get angry; or will you let him know firmly, but kindly, that you don't want to give it up? When you take up for yourself, are you starting fights and quarrels or just honestly expressing how you feel? Can you get what you want without hurting someone? How open should we be in expressing our feelings? Does fear of another person often keep us from saying how we really feel? Could Isaac have said what he felt and still pleased God? What was the reward of Isaac's kindness? What will you do now with the beans? Could you move some of them and share a little of your turf with the person beside you?*

Say, *Jesus told us to: turn the other cheek; love one another; and walk 2 miles if a man forces you to walk 1 mile. In light of what Jesus said, how can you deal with difficult people such as bullies? How can you assert or defend yourself in the right way?*

Use the following role-play[5] (see p. 28) to help the children learn to express themselves in social situations while avoiding aggressive behavior. Tell them what to say in each scene.

- Mary asks to borrow Laura's bracelet for a party. Laura simply says, "Sure." She isn't showing her true feelings and is encouraging Mary to borrow again.
- Act out the scene again. Laura says angrily, "Absolutely not. I don't lend things. I'm surprised you would even ask. Wear your own bracelet."
- Act out the scene again. Laura says, "This bracelet is special to me. It belonged to my grandmother who is dead now. I would rather not lend it."

Discuss the role-play. Ask, **Which of Laura's solutions was best?** Ask additional questions to stimulate further thought about the situation. Let other children play the roles and see what their answers might be.

KINDNESS
(John 8:1-11)

RESOURCES
picture of a woman condemned by the crowd
"stones"

PREPARATION
> Display the teaching picture.

> Dress the following in costume or headpiece: Jesus, the adulterous woman, a few people to represent the crowd.

PROCEDURE
Ask the characters to remain perfectly still and pose a picture (see p. 28) of the scene in John 8:1-11. Jesus can sit on a bench. The woman can stand nearby. Persons in the crowd will point their fingers at her and have large stones in their hands (see p. 14). Ask, **Can you guess who the people are in this scene?** Tell the story:

Jesus was at the temple in Jerusalem, preaching to the people. Scribes and Pharisees brought to him a woman with a bad reputation, a sinner, an adulteress. They reminded Jesus that Jewish law commanded that she be stoned to death for such a sin. Then they asked his opinion. Jesus bent over and started writing with his finger in the sand. They kept

MOLDING

on questioning him. Jesus straightened up and said a very wise thing: "If there is one of you who is not guilty of any sin, you may throw the first stone at her." Once again he bent over and wrote in the sand. When they heard this, the scribes and Pharisees gradually went away, one by one. Then Jesus straightened up and said to the woman, "Where are they? Is there no one left to blame you?" She said, "No one, sir." Then Jesus said, "Neither do I blame you. Go your way, but don't sin again."

Ask, *What is happening? What is each person thinking and feeling? What choice or choices did each person make? What happened as a result of those choices?* Ask children to pose another ending to the story.

Ask, *What does this story teach us about God's love? Each of us needs to learn to condemn only the behavior of someone—not the person herself. Can we be kind to someone whom we know has made a bad mistake? The sinful woman was embarrassed and hurt, and her self-esteem was low. Have you ever seen someone in that situation? How could you help? Are you a kind person? If you've ever needed someone to be kind to you, then you know how it feels to need kindness. What does this story tell us about right living? About reputation? About a good name?*

HELPFULNESS
(Luke 10:38-42)

RESOURCES
Bible
headpieces
large pottery bowl
small bench
wooden spoon

PREPARATION
> Read Luke 10:38-42.

PROCEDURE
Use a tableau (see p. 29) to present the story. Dress characters in headpieces. Martha stands and cradles in her arm a large pottery bowl and wooden spoon. Seat Jesus or Mary on a small bench and the other one on the floor. Ask the children which person they think would be sitting on the bench, based on customs of their day. Decide on other props to put into this scene (see pp. 12-14).

Ask, *Have you ever watched someone you love hurt? I don't mean hurt as in pain in your body, but hurting inside. Maybe your grandparent died, and your parents couldn't stop crying. Maybe your friend lost a pet and grieved for a long time. Maybe the parents of your friend got a divorce, and that hurts a lot.*

Give this background to the story:

Bethany was a small town 2 miles from Jerusalem. Every time Jesus visited there, no matter how much he was hurting inside, he found friends who loved him, cared for him, and comforted him. Their names were Mary, Martha, and Lazarus. With them, Jesus could talk even about his own death. There was another reason why he liked to visit there. The Bible says he didn't really have a home after he left his boyhood home with Mary and Joseph. Luke 9:58 says, "Foxes have holes and birds of the air have nests, but the Son of Man has nowhere to lay his head." Jesus knew what it was like to be homeless. He was always staying with someone else. He had to do that in order to be a preacher of his time. There were no motels or hotels, just a few inns.

When Jesus wanted to visit the home of Mary and Martha, do you think they ever said, "We're too busy," "The house is too dirty," or "We have nothing here to eat?" Instead, they were sure to prepare for him. I suspect he was often a drop-in guest, but they didn't mind that either.

MOLDING

As you tell the story from Luke 10:38-42, ask Martha to step out of the scene at the proper time and say, "Why doesn't she help me? All she wants to do is sit and listen to him. I need help." Then she can return to her place and stand very still again. Ask Mary to step forward at the right time and say, "It's so good to have him here. All I want to do is sit at his feet and listen to his stories." She then will return to the scene. Jesus will step forward and say, "Martha, don't worry so much about feeding us. Just come, sit, and rest and listen." Jesus then returns to the scene. Close the story with discussion. Ask, **Which of the sisters was most helpful to Jesus?** Actually, Jesus loved Martha for attending to details and feeding him. He loved Mary for being thoughtful, listening, and learning.

Ask, *In what ways have you helped someone this week?* Give the children a chance to answer. *Was it because you knew you would get something for helping, or because you really cared? Being helpful is a trait we all need. Are rewards the most important thing in being helpful? Suppose the only reward you get is good feelings about yourself?*

TRUSTWORTHINESS
(Acts 16:16-40)

RESOURCES
costumes
flashlight or "oil lamp"
song "Paul and Silas"
"stocks"
stone-painted paper
window shade

PREPARATION
> Place stone-painted paper on one wall.

PROCEDURE
Turn out the lights in the room. Darken the windows. Use only a small oil lamp or flashlight. If possible, make the room either too hot or too cold.

As the children arrive, ask them to wait in the hall to be brought in one at the time and seated on the floor.

Dress Paul and Silas in costume. Ask them to sit in stocks against the stone wall.

A man in stocks

Say, *In modern-day prisons, men and women are confined to very small rooms called "cells." They hope for good cellmates who will not hurt them, because some prisoners have committed murder, rape, armed robbery, or other violent crimes. They are not usually trustworthy people. Occasionally, if an inmate becomes angry enough to harm someone, he will be put into the "hole," a place where he is completely alone and sees only the people who bring him food.*

One inmate wrote in May 1994: "I know I'm in prison, but I'm happier now than I've ever been in my life. . . . I lived all those years messing up my life. I wish I had put my life in God's hand many years ago. I've missed out on many years of joy. But I'm so happy that He's guiding me now. I'm a completely different man. Praise the Lord!" Explain to the children what it means to "put my life in God's hand."

MOLDING

Tell the following story:

Many years ago in New Testament times, 2 men found themselves sitting in a prison in a city named Philippi. Their "crime" was preaching about Jesus. That prison was worse than prisons are today. It was dark and damp, and often prisoners were chained. Most of the time they did not see the sun. To make matters worse, Paul and Silas' feet were fastened in a wooden frame called "stocks" so they couldn't move them. They were put into the innermost cell, maybe something like "the hole."

At midnight Paul and Silas were singing praises to God. The other prisoners were listening. Suddenly there was a big earthquake, so big that all the doors came open and the chains of the prisoners came unfastened. Paul and Silas's stocks must have broken apart. The jailer was even more terrified than the prisoners. He knew that if anyone escaped, he would be killed because he was responsible for them. But Paul said, "Don't hurt yourself; we're all here." Can you imagine that? They didn't run out of there as fast as they could, even though it was a terrible place. Paul and Silas were trustworthy. They could be trusted to do the right thing.

The jailer called for lights—remember, it was very dark—came in, and asked, "What do I have to do to be saved?" Perhaps the jailer had been listening to their singing in prison and wondered how they could possibly be happy. Then the jailer took Paul and Silas out of that terrible place. They went to the jailer's house where they told everyone there about Jesus. The entire family was baptized. Christians who truly love God can be trusted. Could it be that Paul and Silas didn't run because they wanted to teach others about honesty?

Turn on the lights. Sing a song about Paul and Silas (see p. 173).

Negative Traits

The following lessons can help children see that biblical people didn't always do what was right either, and that sometimes there were unhappy consequences. But help them remember that God can still love us without liking our behavior.

DECEIT
(Luke 22:54-62)

RESOURCES
"campfire"
chalk or felt tip pens
chalk/markerboard or paper
costumes
flashlights
red cellophane paper
"stones" or sticks

PREPARATION
> Move room equipment against the wall.

> Transform the room into a courtyard.

> Darken the room.

> Make a circle of stones or use sticks for a campfire.

PROCEDURE
Dress Peter, a servant girl, and 2 men in headpieces. Have them sit around the fire. Dress a Roman soldier in costume. Have him stand in the background. Use flashlights and red cellophane paper to simulate a fire.

Brainstorm this question: *Your best friend told a secret to someone else that you asked her not to tell. You feel betrayed, deceived, and angry. What will you do now?* The children will present ideas whether or not they're reasonable. Record their answers on a chalk/markerboard or large sheet of paper. Don't allow anyone to say, "That won't work," in response to a suggestion. After evaluating their ideas, tell the story from the Bible.

MOLDING

71

After Jesus observed the Lord's Supper with his disciples, they went to the Mount of Olives. While he was there, a crowd came. In the crowd were Judas, the chief priests, the officers of the temple police, and the elders who had come to arrest him. They took Jesus away to the high priest's house. Peter followed at a distance. The crowd built a fire in the courtyard of the high priest's house, and Peter sat down with them.

Suddenly, a servant girl recognized Peter. She said, "This man was with Jesus." Peter denied it and said, "I don't know Jesus." A little later someone else said, "You also are one of his disciples." Peter replied, "I am not." About an hour later someone said, "Surely you were with Jesus." Peter said, "I don't know what you're talking about." Then Peter heard a rooster crow. Jesus turned and looked at Peter. Peter remembered Jesus' words: "Before the rooster crows today, you will say 3 times that you don't know me." Peter left the courtyard and cried.

Ask, *Does it hurt to be betrayed? Do you have any sympathy for Peter? Why did he do what he did? Do you think he was just plain scared that he might be crucified also? Were the Romans easy to deal with? Remember, they ruled over the Jews and weren't the most popular people in town. Do you think it was an ongoing trait of Peter's to betray his friends? Does anyone know what happened to Peter after this incident?* He became one of the greatest preachers of his time. Tradition says he was crucified upside down, and that's how he died. Peter more than paid for his mistake. *The next time you're tempted to betray a friend, will you think about this story?*

DISHONESTY
(Joshua 7:1-26)

RESOURCES
newspaper clippings pertaining to dishonesty
pencils
word list

PREPARATION
> Ask the children to bring newspaper clippings that pertain to dishonesty, for example, those involving someone who steals something or a public official who keeps money for himself.

> Ask several children to think of examples of honesty and dishonesty. These children will serve on a panel with a leader as moderator.

PROCEDURE
Present several articles from the newspaper on dishonesty.

Present the panel members during large group time. Give each child a minute or so to give an example of honesty and dishonesty. Discuss if honesty means the same thing to everyone. For instance, to some, gambling is dishonest because it's getting something for nothing. To others, it's just a game. When the panel has given its answers to the questions, allow anyone else in the group to give an opinion on honesty. Keep the discussion flowing smoothly.

Tell the following story:

Moses had been a good leader, but now his work was over. His successor was Joshua. God led Joshua and the people to conquer Jericho. God had rules for the takeover. One rule was that the soldiers of Joshua were not to keep anything they took out of the city. Instead, those things were to go into the treasury of the Lord. One of Joshua's men who had helped conquer Jericho broke that rule.

Instead of following God's guidelines, he took some things for himself. Joshua and the people had been very successful in battle. Now, suddenly, that wasn't true. They lost a battle at Ai, and some of the Israelite men were killed. Joshua knew something was wrong, and so he talked to God. God said, "Someone has stolen some things from Jericho."

A search was conducted, tribe by tribe and clan by clan. It was discovered that a man named Aachan had taken a beautiful Babylonian coat and also some silver and gold. He admitted burying them inside his tent. Joshua sent men to search the tent, and they found the things just as Aachan had said. Because of Aachan's dishonesty, he and all his family were killed. All the other people learned a lesson about dishonesty.

Encourage children to ask any questions they may have about the story. Ask: **How important is it that we hang onto "things"?**

Give the children the following word list: tempted, careless, cassette tapes, store, price, hidden, police. Ask each child to write a story using the words. Read aloud several of the stories.

LYING
(Acts 4:37–5:10)

RESOURCES
Bibles (same version)

PREPARATION
> Familiarize yourself with the Bible story.

PROCEDURE
Say, **Close your eyes and think of a time when you had to choose between being truthful or untruthful.** Ask, **Do you agree with this statement? The worst thing about being untruthful is that you have to remember exactly what you said when you lied, or else risk being caught in another lie.**

Ask, **Does anyone have a watch I can borrow? I don't seem to have mine. I'll give it back to you later.**

Say, **Open your Bibles to Acts 4. We're going to do some popcorn Bible reading with this passage. We'll read from Acts 4:37 straight through Acts 5:10. I will call on a child to stand and begin reading. When he/she stops reading, anyone can stand and take up reading where he/she left off. It might even be in the middle of a sentence. That's why you have to watch carefully. It's important that you get the facts from the story as you read.**

Ask the following questions pertaining to good character. Answers are given for leaders.

- What's so amazing about Acts 4:32? (None of the believers felt they owned anything, but that everything belonged to everyone.)
- Read Acts 4:32-35 silently. How would you compare the dedication of New Testament believers to God and our dedication to God?
- If all the wealth in this world were redivided, is it possible we might not have homeless people and the poor all around us? Does that seem like the right thing to do?
- Read Acts 5:1-2. Two people weren't willing to share. Who were they? (Ananias and Sapphira)
- Go back to Acts 4:32. Who told the Christians they had to share? (no one) Did God tell them sharing was their duty, or was it their idea? (They wanted to share.)
- According to Acts 5:5, what happened to Ananias because of his failure to obey the rules? (He died.)
- Look in Acts 5:2, 7-9. Who was in on the secret plot? (Ananias' wife, Sapphira)
- Does this story mean that if we lie, we will die immediately? What does God want us to learn from this story about truthfulness?
- See Acts 5:11. What did this experience do to the rest of the people in the church? (There was great fear.)

MOLDING

73

Refuse to return the watch you borrowed. See the reactions of the owner and everyone else in the room. Ask, *Did I ever say I would give the watch back? Which is worse: promising to give it back and not doing it, or not promising anything and not giving it back? In either case, am I still being dishonest?*

UNGRATEFULNESS
(Luke 17:11-19)

RESOURCES
ragged costume
rags

PREPARATION
> Familiarize yourself with the Bible story.

PROCEDURE
Send one child to the Searching Stop to find out all she can about lepers. Dress a child as a leper. He will wear a very simple ragged costume. He might have rags tied on his hands, arms, and legs to hide his leprosy. Seat him near the leader. Say, *If you were going to visit lepers, what would you want to know about leprosy before you got there? _____ is going to tell us what she found out.* Make sure the following information is included: *As they came near the people, lepers were required to call out loudly, "Unclean," "Unclean." which warned the crowd to move away.* Ask the child dressed as a leper, to call out these words. Tell the story of Jesus healing the ten lepers.

Jesus was on his way to Jerusalem. As he entered a village, 10 lepers came near him. Leprosy was a terrible skin disease, and persons who had leprosy were forced to live apart from others. Sores covered parts of the body that were infected. Fingers and toes disappeared as the disease ate away the skin. The lepers called out to Jesus from a distance, "Jesus, Master, have mercy on us." They had heard stories about him healing the sick. Jesus said to them, "Go and show yourselves to the priest." What a strange thing to say!

As the lepers walked away, they noticed their leprosy was gone. When one of the lepers saw that he was well, he turned around and praised God with a loud voice. Then the man, who was a Samaritan, fell at Jesus' feet and thanked him for good health. Then Jesus asked, "Where are the other 9? Have none of them said thank you to God?" Then Jesus said to the grateful man: "Go your way; you were healed because you believed it could happen."

Ask the children to keep their Bibles open to Luke 17:11-19 and to stand and take one step forward when they think they have the answer to the following questions. Answers are given for leaders.

* Call out some sad words or phrases in this story. Call out some happy words or phrases.
* Why did Jesus say, "Go and show yourselves to the priests?" Look up Matthew 8:4 for help with the answer. (Because a priest had to declare a leper healed before the leper could live with other people)
* Who thanked Jesus, and who didn't? (1 leper thanked him; the others didn't.) In Luke 17:16, why does the Bible writer put in the phrase, "And he was a Samaritan?" (Jews considered Samaritans foreigners or outcasts.)
* Can you sense the disappointment in Jesus' voice in Luke 17:17-19?
* What disease today can make people feel as hopeless as having leprosy? (AIDS)

Say, *Close your eyes and think of a time when you forgot to say, "Thank you." Who did you disappoint? Could you still say it or write a thank-you note? Would doing so make you feel better? Would you be proud of yourself, or would you feel so deserving of what was done for you that you wouldn't have to say, "Thank you?"*

MOLDING

Notes

[1] A wonderful resource for studying biblical heroes and subsequent character formation is the *BibLearn Series on Biblical Personalities* (Nashville: Broadman Press).

[2] See *The Greatness That Was Babylon* (New York: Hawthorne Books, Inc., 1962) 173.

[3] Adapted from Peter Farb, *The Land, Wildlife, and Peoples of the Bible* (New York: Harper & Row, 1967) 108, 109.

[4] Adapted from Bruce Joyce and Marsha Weily, *Models of Teaching* (Needham MA: Allyn & Bacon, 1986) 193.

[5] Ibid., 386.

MOLDING

Chapter 8
REENACTING: Enjoying Jewish Traditions

Rationale

Traditions are customs or practices handed down through generations. Jewish life was rich in tradition and long-standing religious practices. Ancient customs were part of Jewish daily life. In this chapter children will learn about some of these customs through planning and participating in a synagogue worship service, a dinner with a wealthy Pharisee, a Palestinian village, and a marketplace.

Worship at the Synagogue

RESOURCES
Bible headpieces
"chest"
costumes
fabric
felt tip pens
"menorah"
paper
pencils
"prayer shawls"
reading stand
"scrolls"
"shophar"
stone-painted wall and floor
Synagogue Worksheets
trombones
trumpets
yarmulkes

PREPARATION

> Invite parents and siblings to the service.

> Select biblical headpieces for everyone in the class and full costumes for leaders in the service. In some synagogues, all men and boys wore prayer shawls (see p. 33), but you might provide them just for those children leading the service. Prayer shawls were made of cotton, wool, or silk, bordered by fringe on the ends. They were long and narrow, coming almost to the knees. Often they were pulled up over the head as a headcovering. Some men and boys wore yarmulkes (see p. 33) that fit on the back of their heads.

> Arrange the room like a synagogue. Make plenty of space in the center of the room. In biblical times people sat on benches. For this service, however, the children and leaders can sit on the floor. Place stone-painted paper (see p. 14) on the walls and floor. At the front, place a

The Synagogue Service

77

small reading stand, a storage chest for the scrolls, and a 7-branched lampstand (menorah).

> Borrow trombones and trumpets.[2]

> Borrow or make a shophar (see p. 13)

> Have available many scrolls.

> Prepare Synagogue Worksheets (see p. 85).

> Read Luke 4:16-30, Acts 18:8, Mark 5:22, 23.

> Appoint a child to be the rosh-ha-keneseth. Ask him to prepare his own sermon. Give him suggestions for the length of it. For help, see "The Sermon" in the role-play of the worship service.

> Appoint a child to be the hazan.

> Appoint a child to be Jesus for the reading from the prophets.

> Appoint a child to pray the Tefillah, or prayer of praise.

> Appoint a child to read the Scripture lesson from the Torah.

PROCEDURE

Choose children who will portray men, women, and children. Dress them in appropriate headpieces and/or costumes. Just before the service begins, ask them to exit the room and then to re-enter in separate groups of men and women. Those playing the part of children will sit with the women, except for boys 12 years or older.

Say, **The main purpose of a synagogue was not for public worship but for teaching people the scriptures. It was also used for funerals and social events, as a place for people to discuss matters of the community, as a courtroom, and as a synagogue school for the boys. But on the Sabbath, worship services were held in**

synagogues. No sacrifices were made at synagogues. People had to go to the Temple at Jerusalem to offer sacrifices.

On the Sabbath the community ceased all work and attended the synagogue services. There were 4 Sabbath services: Friday at sundown, Saturday morning (the main service for the whole family), Saturday afternoon, and Saturday at sundown.

The man in charge of the service was the rosh-ha-keneseth, the "ruler" or "leader" of the synagogue. He sat with the elders on a platform behind the reading stand. Behind the platform was a curtain, and behind this, the chest holding the scrolls. The scrolls were wrapped in embroidered linen covers.

The hazan, or attendant, cared for the synagogue building. Often he lived there. He had several duties. He instructed the boys and girls in reading, blew the trumpet from the rooftop to let people know it was the beginning of the Sabbath, and took special care of the scrolls. It was he who took the scroll from the chest, unwound the cloth that covered it, and handed it to the person who was going to read or sing it during the service. When the reader finished it, the hazan rewound it in the cloth and returned it to its place. The Sabbath morning service began with the blowing of the shophar, a ram's horn[1] (see p. 13).

Have the children role-play the following parts of a worship service:

The hazan gives one blast on the shophar at the same time another individual gives one blast on a trumpet. The worshipers enter. Read Psalm 92 and 93.

- *The Invocation*: The rosh-ha-keneseth leads in reciting the Shema (Deuteronomy 6:4, 5): "Hear, O Israel: The Lord is our God, the Lord alone. You shall love the Lord your God with all your heart, and with all your soul, and with all your might."

• *The Tefillah*: The rosh-ha-keneseth calls on a member of the synagogue to stand in front of the chest containing the scrolls and to lead in a prayer praising God.

• *The Scripture Lesson*: The hazan takes the scroll from the chest and hands it to the reader. The scripture lesson taken from the Torah is then read. (In biblical times this was done only by a male member of the congregation over age 13. If priests or Levites were known to be present, they were given the opportunity to read.) The reader hands the scroll back to the hazan, who puts it in the chest. The reader then sits down.

• *Reading from the Prophets*: The rosh-ha-keneseth asks a member of the congregation or a visitor to come forward and read a portion from the prophets. He introduces the reader as "Jesus, son of Joseph." The hazan hands the scroll of the prophet Isaiah to the reader. He reads aloud: "The spirit of the Lord is upon me, because he has anointed me to bring good news to the poor. He has sent me to promise release to the captives and recovery of sight to the blind, to let the oppressed go free, to proclaim the year of the Lord's favor." Jesus rolls the scroll up and gives it back to the hazan and then sits down. He then tells them that this scripture is speaking about him. People in the synagogue start whispering to each other about him because he is claiming to be the Son of God. (Remember, Jesus had lived all his growing-up years in Nazareth and attended the synagogue regularly with his family. It was a very small village, so he was no stranger; they knew him well).

• *The Sermon*: While seated, the rosh-ha-keneseth presents a sermon that helps the people understand the scriptures and how to live better lives. The rosh-ha-keneseth may invite someone else to preach the sermon for the day.

• *The Close*: The rosh-ha-keneseth asks for the congregation to stand for a closing prayer. He says: "The Lord bless you and keep you. The Lord look kindly upon you and be gracious to you. The Lord bestow his favor upon you and give you peace. Shalom." He then asks each person in the synagogue to turn to his neighbor on either side and say, "Peace be with you." Neighbors respond, "And also with you."[3]

Hand out the "Synagogue Worksheet" (see p. 85) to be completed by the children.

Dinner with a Wealthy Pharisee

RESOURCES
bagels
basin
bedsheet
Bible headpieces
bowls
cassette tape player
chair
cheese
chicken
colorful pillows
costumes
cups
dates
fig bars
fish
lamb
matzos (Jewish wafers)
melons
"oil lamps"
olives
quail
serving dishes
tape of Jewish folk songs
tomatoes
towels
water

PREPARATION
> Assign foods for children and leaders to bring.

> Secure costumes for the host and 3 servants.

REENACTING

> Arrange the room like a wealthy person's home. Place room equipment against the walls. Scatter colorful pillows around the room. Place a large, square cloth such as a bedsheet on the floor. Place bowls, cups, and serving dishes on top of the cloth. Display several oil lamps (see p. 12).

PROCEDURE

Choose a child to be the host. Dress him in an elegant costume. Choose 3 children to be servants. Dress them in simple costumes. Appoint the other children and the leaders to be dinner guests. Give them biblical headpieces.

As the children enter the room, ask them to observe these Jewish customs: (1) remove their shoes; (2) exchange bows, greetings, and kisses with the host. Ask a servant to give each child a drink of water. Ask another servant to seat the guests in turn, pour water on their feet over a basin, rub their feet with his hands, and then wipe their feet with the towel hanging from his belt.

Ask the guests to remain barefoot and to lie on the floor around the sheet, reclining on one elbow and eating with the other hand, with feet stretched out behind them. This stance represents the guests reclining on couches in biblical times. Play a tape of Jewish folk songs in the background.

Ask 2 servants to offer guests small pieces of melon, cheese, dates, fig bars, olives, tomatoes, bagels, matzos, and meat. Explain that this dinner was quite different from those Jesus had in his home growing up, for his was a poor family and a simple home, and the poor rarely ate meat. Ask the children what they think these guests would be talking about. Ask them to try to talk to the persons sitting next to them about those subjects.

After a time of conversation, share the following information with the children as they continue eating:

The host always sat facing the door. The seats of honor were on the right and left of the host. Sometimes the guests had quarrels over which one was the greatest and deserved the best seats (can you imagine that?) and the host would settle the argument.

Jesus once talked about these seats of honor. He was trying to say one's seating position at the table didn't make him great. One who was really great must be a humble person who worked to serve and help others. Once Jesus washed his disciples' feet to illustrate this. Look up John 13:1-14 in your Bible. Which disciple did not want Jesus to wash his feet? Do you think he ever understood what Jesus was trying to do? On one occasion, Jesus used an opportunity like this to scold the Pharisees.

Dinners or banquets were held at night, and the rooms were brightly lighted. An uninvited guest was cast into the darkness.[4] Ask the children to pantomime how to deal with a "gate crasher."

A Palestinian Village

RESOURCES
crayons
felt tip pens
manger
masking tape
paintbrushes
pans for cooking
pencils
table paper
tempera paint
water jars

PREPARATION

> Remove everything from the walls of the classroom.

> Print the following questions on a sheet of paper:

- What did a synagogue look like on the outside?
- What did women use to grind grain?
- How did donkeys look when weighted down with bundles to carry?
- What was the city well like?
- What did the trunks and branches of palm trees look like?
- How did fig trees look?
- What were Jewish houses like on the outside?
- What did the men carry their lunch in each day?
- What kind of fuel did the women use for their ovens?
- How were the outside ovens or open cookfires made?
- What was a city gate like?
- How did women spin and weave wool?

PROCEDURE
(may require several class sessions)

Ask several children to go to the Searching Stop to find the answers to the question list. They may use Bible encyclopedias, dictionaries, illustrated books, and other reference materials.

Ask the other children to cut pieces of doubled white table paper the length of each wall, and then to tape lengths together as needed.

Assemble the group. Explain how to make a panorama, or a scene that moves around in a continuous circle. To help plan the scenes, ask the researchers to report their findings from the Searching Stop. Compile and display the following list to give ideas to all of the children:

- Houses built around a courtyard
- Families sharing outdoor ovens and grain mills
- Women carrying babies and water jars, holding the hands of young children
- People waving to each other and stopping to talk
- Young children playing games such as hopscotch, catch, wrestling, hide-and-seek, and ring toss
- Olives and grapes drying on rooftops
- Children playing on rooftoops

- Boys on their way to synagogue school carrying pens, tablets or papyrus sheets, and their lunches in a leather bag and wearing phylacteries (see pp. 119, 120) on their arms and yarmulkes (see p. 33) on their heads
- Fathers on their way to work carrying their lunches in leather bags and water in goatskin bags (see p. 14)
- Roman soldiers (see p. 32)
- Sheep and goats
- Donkeys (see p. 12) carrying heavy loads and perhaps 2 large baskets on either side of their heads and other things piled on top of their backs, some tied outside their houses to keep them from running away
- Women and girls bringing fuel in for the ovens on a donkey (see p. 107)
- The outside of the synagogue and people going in and out
- Beggars, including the blind and lame
- Women and girls grinding grain on a hand mill (see p. 107)
- The city well and cisterns for catching rain water
- People too sick to stand; the elderly, bent and stooped
- A city gate
- The city wall with soldiers stationed on top
- Palm and fig trees
- Birds, pigeons
- Older men with gray beards, young men with dark beards
- Women and girls cooking over an open fire outside or in an outdoor oven (see p. 108)
- Families walking together
- Women with large, round, flat baskets of olives on their heads
- Women and girls spinning wool and weaving outside
- Children climbing a hill
- Camels being led down the street
- Chickens and roosters
- Women and girls making baskets

Ask the children to trace around each other and their leaders while they are standing next to the paper in various poses or lying on the paper, making sure to draw both side and back views. Remind them to include persons of all ages, shapes, and sizes. Then have the children draw biblical costumes on the figures.

Attach the panorama to the wall. Place some inanimate objects on the floor at the bottom of the scene to give it realism, for example, a few water jars, a manger, and pans for cooking. Ask the children to share their perceptions about the scene.

A Marketplace

RESOURCES
booths
clothes drying racks
costumes
"gold and silver coins"
folding tables
pillows
rugs
tape of Jewish folk songs
"SHOP" signs
supplies for booths

PREPARATION
> Invite parents, siblings, and friends to visit the marketplace.

PROCEDURE
(may require several class sessions)

Ask several children to sit for a few minutes where two busy halls intersect in your building. Ask them to observe the hustle and bustle of the crowds, noise level, new information, what the people are carrying in their hands, and so on. When the children return, ask them to report to the large group. Say, *That's what it would have been like to be in the marketplace when a caravan came through the town.*

Help the children understand the importance of the marketplace for the Jewish people. Say, *Once or twice a year caravans from faraway places brought jewelry, rugs, leather, perfume, and*

silks to sell to local merchants in the market-place. They also brought world news.[5] *The marketplace was more than just a place to buy and sell. It was a good place for recreation, discussing current events, and getting the latest news.*

The potter was one of the most important merchants in the marketplace. He made the bowls, pots, water jars, storage jars, and cooking vessels that were used every day in Jewish homes. At the end of the day one could hear in the marketplace the clinking jars and pots on the donkey's back as the potter slowly trudged home, disappointed with not having sold all his goods.

The silversmith made jewelry, candlesticks, musical instruments, and money. The coppersmith furnished trays, dishes, pots, pans, kettles, vases, and pitchers. Among the fruits and vegetables sold were: melons, cucumbers, olives, tomatoes, dates, figs, beans and peas, and pistachio and almond nuts. There was no refrigeration, so cooks probably shopped the marketplace every day.

The seller of grain placed his cloak on the ground and then poured his product out in a mound on his cloak and measured the grain carefully for the buyer. It was a custom that each measure must run over. The buyer held the wide skirt of his cloak to receive the grain. Jesus must have watched this many times when he was growing up, because, as an adult, he once said: "Give, and it will be given to you. A good measure, pressed down, shaken together, running over, will be put into your lap; for the measure you give will be the measure you get back." What do you think he meant by that?

Instead of buying and selling, some people in the village swapped such items as a chicken for a water jar. Doves (pigeons) were also sold in the marketplace.[6]

Appoint several children to bring supplies for booths. Appoint others to be the sellers. Maybe 2 children will want to work together on a booth, or 1 or more children may wish to share a booth with a leader. Leaders can serve as advisors. Talk with the children about negotiating for products and services.

Share this information concerning use of money in biblical times: *There were several commonly used silver coins: the shekel, drachma, stater, and the denarius. A denarius or 2 staters were wages for a day's work. The denarius was a Roman coin. The coin most used in New Testament times was the shekel. At one time the cost of a slave was 30 shekels. Judas betrayed Jesus for 30 pieces of silver, or about 30 shekels. A copper coin called the "lepton" or the "mite" was the least valuable of all coins. Do you remember when Jesus observed the widow with "the widow's mite"? There was also a coin of very little value called the "far-thing." Coins were made of silver, gold, copper, or bronze. They were constantly changing in value.*[7]

Ask the children to make gold and silver coins for shopping (see p. 12). Let them decide what they will charge for each item at the time of the sale without regard to the particular value of coins.

Appoint children to walk through the crowd dressed in simple costumes and to role-play the following characters: the frantic Mary and Joseph searching for the lost Jesus, Roman soldiers, shepherds, well-dressed Pharisees, women with empty baskets for shopping or water jars on top of their heads, a waterseller with a goatskin water bag slung over his back, lepers crying out "Unclean! Unclean!" as people scatter, a blind beggar sitting and asking for coins.

Remove items from the room that don't fit into a marketplace scene.

Play the tape of Jewish folk songs.

Have the children construct booths. Portable clothes drying racks and folding tables can be used to hold items. Rugs and pillows can be used by some merchants to display their wares on the ground. Ask the children to set up some of the following booths and to display signs above each booth.

- Woodworking
- Fish
- Pottery
- Baked Goods
- Rope
- Fruits and vegetables
- Fabrics
- Poultry and meat
- Spices and herbs
- Tax collector
- Grain seller
- Coppersmith
- Silversmith
- Basket weaver

As parents and friends enter the marketplace, hand out coins for purchasing items. Each visitor to the marketplace is required to pay something to the tax collector! You might place the name "Matthew" above the tax collector's booth. Buyers and sellers can negotiage prices.

Notes

[1]Adapted from John c. Cochran, *Learning about Bible Places of Worship* (Nashville: Convention Press, 1980) 35-37. Used by permission.

[2]Ibid., 36.

[3]Synagogue service information adapted from *Exploring 2 for Leaders* (Nashville: The Sunday School Board of the Southern Baptist Convention, August 1990). All rights reserved. Used by permission.

[4]Eating customs adapted from Fred Wight, *Manners and Customs of Bible Lands* (Chicago: Moody Press, 1953) 69-79; and "Eating Customs of the Poor and Wealthy, in *Exploring 2 Kit for Leaders* (Nashville: The Sunday School Board of the Southern Baptist Convention, August 1990). All rights reserved. Used by permission.

[5]Marketplace information adapted from Marion C. Armstrong, "A Spice Caravan," in *Life and Customs in Bible Times* (Nashville: Abingdon Press, 1943) 18.

[6]Ibid., *Workers in Bible Times* (Nashville: Abingdon Press, 1943) 13, 15, 23.

[7]Information on Bible coins adapted from Betty Goetz and Ruth Bomberger, *Marketplace, 29 A.D.: A Bible Times Experience* (Stevensville MI: B. J. Goetz Publishing Co., 1989) 85.

REENACTING

Synagogue Worksheet

Circle the answer that completes each statement.

(1) The ruler of the synagogue was _____.
    the boss   the rosh-ha-kneset   the master of ceremonies

(2) _____ blew the shophar.
    a trumpet player   the hazan   a local farmer

(3) Young boys and girls sat _____.
    with the men   with the women   underneath the balcony

(4) Scrolls were kept _____.
    on a table   in a chest   on the piano

(5) _____ took care of the building.
    the janitor   the hazan   a paid servant girl

(6) _____ was used before the invocation.
    an opening prayer   the Psalms   the book of Genesis   the book of Matthew

(7) The tefillah was _____.
    the preacher's hat   the opening prayer   the chest that held the scrolls

(8) The scripture lesson came from _____.
    the Ten Commandments   the Torah   the Sermon on the Mount

(9) When Jesus was invited to read from the prophets, he read from _____.
    Luke   Revelation   Isaiah

(10) A sermon was _____ given.
    never   always   sometimes

(11) At the close of the service, _____.
    the ruler of the synagogue led a closing prayer   they took an offering   everyone rushed out

Chapter 9
CELEBRATING: Observing Special Seasons

Rationale

The Jewish people loved to celebrate. They had many special feasts. Their feast days were not solemn occasions, but fun-filled times of joyous celebration. The Feast of the Passover was one such special time. It began with a pilgrimage to Jerusalem.

Children should understand the significance of celebrating as Christians. In this chapter's activities they will learn about the importance of some Jewish events and experience a celebration of them. They also will participate in observances of the Christian seasons of Advent and Lent.

A Pilgrimage to Jerusalem

RESOURCES
cassette player
cassette tape of Jewish folk songs
paper
pencils
song "Shalom, Chaverim"

PREPARATION
> Make copies of the lyrics on the tape.

PROCEDURE
Present this background information[1]:

One of the happiest times for Jewish families was when they went to the Temple in Jerusalem to celebrate feasts such as the Passover. The roads to Jerusalem were always crowded, but especially during one of the religious feast times. All Jews wanted to visit the great Temple at least once in their lifetime. First they packed their sleeping mats, some food, and a few clothes. All the families traveled together in a caravan for safety on the road. First in the procession were the older men, and then the younger men. Donkeys and camels followed, carrying old people who couldn't walk very well. Last in the procession were the women and children. The people sang as they walked together. The children played with friends, cousins, brothers, and sisters. They enjoyed grandparents, aunts, and uncles. When they stopped for the night, each family built a campfire. They probably ate vegetable stew and bread. They fed and watered their animals. Perhaps they danced the "Hora," a Jewish dance we will learn right now.

Move room equipment against the walls, or find a larger open space. Play a tape of Jewish folk songs, beginning with a slow tempo and speeding up gradually. Say, *Form a large circle. Face the center. Join hands.* Give these instructions repeatedly: *Step to the left side with your left foot. Cross your right foot in back. Put your weight on your right foot. Step to the left with your left foot. Hop on it. Swing your right foot across the front. Step on your right foot. Hop on it. Swing your left foot across in front.*

Families probably sang together before bedtime. Sing a song from the tape. *Then they got out their sleeping mats and went to sleep under the stars. The next morning they ate a breakfast of bread, cheese, fruit, and milk. They began traveling again. At lunchtime they stopped under the shade of big trees and ate a lunch of cheese and dates, flat cakes of bread, and melons. You could hear the laughter and singing of the people all over the hills and valleys. The next night they may have camped at Jericho.*

Their legs ached as they started climbing into the mountains near Jerusalem. As they got near the city, they saw the top of the gold and white marble Temple, gleaming in the sunlight. They began to sing "Songs of Ascents" found in Psalms 120–134. When they arrived in Jerusalem, many of them stayed with friends or relatives. But thousands of them slept in tents surrounding the city. Each day the families went to the Temple for the Passover feast—or whatever feast was in progress. They saw many priests in white robes. They prayed and listened to musical instruments. They stayed a week in Jerusalem, and then they started back home. Every year the families looked forward to those wonderful trips! They probably sang a song together as they left Jerusalem. Perhaps they met new friends in Jerusalem to whom it was hard to say goodbye. Sing "Shalom, Chaverim" (see p. 171).

Something surprising happened on one of those trips when Jesus was 12 years old. He had gone with his family to Jerusalem to celebrate the Feast of the Passover. The trip from Nazareth to Jerusalem was about 80 miles. On foot, it took 3 or 4 days to complete. The festival ended, and all the travelers started home. The group had traveled about a day when, suddenly, Mary and Joseph missed Jesus. Perhaps one of Jesus' brothers, sisters, or friends came to his parents and said, "We can't find Jesus." It was a parent's worst nightmare. Mary and Joseph looked for him among their relatives and friends. Then they went back to Jerusalem, a day's journey. Suppose Mary and Joseph arrived back there after sunset. Wouldn't the heavy doors in the city wall be closed and the iron bars be in place?

For 3 days Mary and Joseph searched the city, frantically looking for Jesus. What do you suppose Mary and Joseph thought about during that time? With whom did Jesus stay? Where did he sleep and eat? Perhaps the city was not quite so crowded since the festival was over. Mary and Joseph found Jesus sitting in the Temple with the religious teachers. He was listening to them, asking them questions, and, to everyone's astonishment, he was answering some of their questions. His mother said, "Why have you treated us like this? Your father and I have been very worried." Jesus gave a strange answer: "Why were you looking for me? Didn't you know that I must be in my Father's house?" What do you suppose he meant by that? Mary and Joseph did not understand either. They left Jerusalem and started home again with Jesus. But Mary and Joseph didn't forget about his answer to their question.

Jesus was the oldest child in the family. His brothers and sisters are mentioned in Mark 6:2-3. Do you think they were on the trip? Were Jesus' grandparents on the trip? Do you think they were as worried as his parents?

What is the main thing you and I can learn from this story about Jesus? This is the only story we have from Jesus' childhood. What does it tell you about him as a child?

Distribute pencil and paper. Ask the children to write a sensational headline for this story, for example, "Child Lost, Parents Frantic." Read some of these aloud.

Ask, *How did Joseph and the other men get off work to go to the Feasts? Did they work from 8 to 5 each day with an hour off for lunch?* Some of them had their own businesses, like Joseph who was a carpenter. Perhaps he just closed his shop for a week. Jewish males were required to attend the Passover Feast, so in the whole community, shops probably closed and businesses shut down.

Say, *You're going to a feast in Jerusalem. What will you take with you? List your answers on the same sheet on which you wrote a sensational headline. Compare lists to see if you are thinking alike.*

Passover

RESOURCES
Bible headpieces
"bitter herbs"
cups
grape juice
ingredients for kharoset (see recipe)
instructions for seder meal
matzos
paper
pencil
roast lamb
tape of Jewish folk songs

Kharoset

2 apples
½ c. white raisins
½ c. pecans
½ tsp. cinnamon
1 TBS. vinegar
¼ c. honey

Wash and core apples. Grind apples, raisins, and nuts together. Stir in cinnamon, vinegar, and honey.

PREPARATION
> Read Exodus 2:23; 11; 12; Mark 14:12-16, 26; Luke 22:7-13.

> Make copies of instructions for a seder meal.

> Prepare a simple seder (Passover) meal.

PROCEDURE
Present this background information[2]:

The Hebrew word for Passover is "pesah," which means "passing over." Passover marked the deliverance of the Hebrews from Egyptian slavery. God commanded the people to keep the feast as a memorial always. Jesus celebrated it throughout his lifetime. In fact, he celebrated it with his disciples just before he died.

The Feast of the Passover was celebrated for a week in the spring, around March or April. It was the first of the 3 great religious festivals and the most important of all the Jewish annual feasts. It began on the evening of the first day with a family meal known as the seder, meaning "order of service." The meal consisted of specially prepared foods such as the "paschal lamb," unleavened bread, bitter herbs, and wine.

The lamb was to be prepared in accordance with God's instructions. It had to be less than a year old, male, and perfect. In Egypt, the blood of the lamb had been sprinkled on the lintels and doorposts of the houses to protect the Hebrews from the death angel. Their homes were "passed over" and their firstborn sons spared when the angel saw the blood. Later, when Passover was celebrated in Caanan, the blood was sprinkled on the altar. As the people killed the animal, they prayed for forgiveness of their sins. The unleavened bread symbolized the haste with which the Hebrews' departed from Egypt, allowing no time for the bread "to rise." The Jews dipped parsley into salt water to help them remember the tears of their ancestors. This action symbolized the bitter life the Hebrews endured as slaves in Egypt.

At the close of the Passover meal, the Jews sang Psalms 115–118. Jesus and his disciples also sang after the Passover meal. See Mark 14:26.

Jewish families of today still observe Passover Week. It begins at sundown on the 14th day of Nisan and is celebrated for 8 days. It includes prayer, scripture reading, and recalling the deliverance of the Jews from Egypt. The families remove from their homes all grain products containing wheat, rye, barley, or oats to ensure that all leaven, or yeast, is out of the house. They use dishes and utensils that have never been touched by food with leaven. Then those are packed away and used only at Passover the next year.

The families eat roast lamb, bitter herbs, horseradish, parsley, and an unleavened bread called "matzos." A dish of chopped apples and nuts, called "kharoset," is also served. This food represents the mortar of the bricks the Hebrews were forced to make in Egypt. A roasted egg was added later as a symbol for mourning.

Explain that the class will now eat a seder meal. Ask each person to wear a biblical headpiece. Appoint a host and his youngest son. Give each of them a copy of the following model[3] for the meal. Appoint all other children to serve as guests.

Direct the following role-play:

- The host pours the first cup of grape juice and recites a prayer: "Blessed art Thou, O Lord our God, who has created the fruit of the vine. Blessed art Thou, O Lord our God, who has sustained us and enabled us to reach this season."
- The host washes his hands. The parsley is dipped into salt water and then passed around the table. Then the food is removed. The host pours the second cup of grape juice.
- The youngest son asks the following questions: "Why is this night different from all other nights? On other nights we eat leavened bread, but on this night only unleavened bread. On this night we eat only bitter herbs. Why do we dip herbs twice? On other nights we eat meat roasted, stewed, or boiled, but on this night why only roasted meat?"
- The father explains Jewish history beginning with Abraham and ending with the Hebrews' deliverance from Egypt. The food is brought back in. The father explains about the lamb, bitter herbs, and unleavened bread.
- The group sings Psalms 113-114 and drinks the second cup of grape juice.
- The host washes his hands a second time. He breaks off pieces of the unleavened bread and blesses them. He then takes the bread and bitter herbs and dips them in the sweet kharoset mixture and gives them to each person.
- Everyone eats the roasted (paschal) lamb.
- After supper, the host pours the third cup of grape juice, representing the blood of the Passover lamb. He says another special blessing, and everyone drinks from the cup. (You may prefer not to have the children drink from a common cup.)
- The group recites Psalms 115–118 and drinks the 4th cup of grape juice.
- The group sings a closing hymn beginning with "All thy works shall praise Thee, Jehovah, our God" and concluding with "From everlasting to everlasting Thou art God, and besides Thee, we have no King, Redeemer or Savior."

Advent

RESOURCES

appliance box (large)
Bibles
biblical headpieces
bow
Christmas cards (nonsecular)
Christmas gift wrap (nonsecular)
cookies
costumes
doll
flashlight
gift boxes (small)
"gifts" (to resemble gold, frankincense, myrrh)
glue
hot chocolate
hot plate or electric skillet
ingredients for cookies (see recipes)
painting of donkeys and sheep
paper
pencils
posterboard, green
ribbon
songs: "Timothy's Carol" and "Sing Hosannas"
swaddling clothes
unit banner

No-Bake Cookie Krispies

1 tsp. butter
1 c. sugar
2 eggs (well-beaten)
1 c. finely cut dates
2 c. Rice Krispies
1 c. chopped nuts
1 c. coconut

Heat first 4 ingredients in a skillet for 5-7 minutes. Add Rice Krispies and nuts. Stir. Moisten hands in cold water. Shape mixture into balls. Roll in coconut. Place on cookie sheet to cool.

No-Bake Chocolate Cookies

2 c. sugar
3 TBS. cocoa
½ c. butter
½ c. milk
2 c. quick oatmeal
½ c. peanut butter
1 tsp. vanilla

Put oatmeal and peanut butter in large bowl and set aside. Combine sugar, cocoa, butter, and milk in pan or electric skillet and bring to a boil. When mixture reaches a rolling boil, cook for 1 minute and 10 seconds. Remove from heat. Add vanilla. Pour chocolate sauce over oatmeal and peanut butter. Mix well. Drop by teaspoon quickly onto wax paper. Cool.

PREPARATION

> Try to arrange a trip to someone's barn where you can tell the Christmas story and afterwards serve hot chocolate and cookies. Or, use the appliance box as a stable.

> Make a unit title banner out of Christmas gift wrap (no Santa Claus paper, please).

> Display a drawing of the heads and necks of donkeys and sheep (see p. 12).

> Display the following statement: "People are always happy to hear about the coming birth of a child."

> Write the following statements on strips of paper. Answers are provided for leaders.

- Joseph and Mary travel to Bethlehem. (4)
- The shepherds go to Bethlehem to see the baby. (8)
- Jesus is born and laid in a manger. (6)
- Joseph discovers he has to go to Bethlehem to register for a census. (3)
- Joseph is engaged to Mary, a girl from Nazareth. (1)
- Many angels announce the birth to shepherds. (7)
- Joseph and Mary choose a cave to sleep in. (5)
- An angel appears to Mary to tell her she's going to have a baby. (2)

> Review the following background information: Jewish marriage customs played a significant role in the Christmas story (see pp. 105, 106). During their engagement period Joseph found out Mary was pregnant. An engagement was considered final and was witnessed by the families of the bride and groom. They were called

man and wife. To seal the promise, the groom gave the bride a gold ring or a written document. This was not the same as the wedding, which came about a year later. Puzzled, Joseph wanted to break the engagement. Maybe he lay awake for a long time thinking about what he should do. According to Jewish law, he could get a bill of divorce without specifying the reason. But an angel urged him to "take Mary as your wife." Men were not allowed to act as midwives so, at Jesus' birth, Mary "brought forth her first-born son" herself. The women prided themselves on self-delivery.

PROCEDURE
(may require several sessions)

Have the children face the cave/stable. Ask, *What is another word for Advent?* Coming. Say, *Advent begins the 4th Sunday before Christmas and ends at midnight on Christmas Eve. It is the time for waiting and preparing for Christmas. The color purple is used in Advent decorations because it is the color of kings. We light candles on Advent wreaths and also decorate Chrismon trees.*

Point to the statement on the wall. Ask, *Is that statement true? When wouldn't it be true? Was the announcement we talk about today a happy one? Why were Mary and Joseph concerned when they learned Mary was pregnant? But an angel spoke to both of them and told them to get ready because this baby needed a home. After some doubts they had at first, Mary and Joseph were very happy that they were going to have a child, and they got married. Mary was so happy, in fact, that she sang a beautiful praise song to God. It went something like this:*

My soul magnifies the Lord, and my spirit rejoices in God my Savior, for he has looked with favor on the lowliness of his servant. Surely, from now on all generations will call me blessed; for the Mighty one has done great

things for me, and holy is his name. His mercy is for those who fear him from generation to generation. He has shown strength with his arm; he has scattered the proud in the thoughts of their hearts. He has brought down the powerful from their thrones, and lifted up the lowly; he has filled the hungry with good things, and sent the rich away empty. He has helped his servant Israel, in remembrance of his mercy, according to the promise he made to our ancestors, to Abraham and to his descendants forever.

Ask, *Does that song sound familiar to you? Perhaps you remember it from the story of Hannah. Turn to 1 Samuel 2:1-10 and Luke 1:46-55. Can you hold your Bibles open at both places and compare them? What was Hannah so happy about?*

Mary of Nazareth and Gabriel

Say, *Mary and Joseph came from Nazareth, a village that was not very well known. In fact, there is no mention of it in the Old Testament. It was an 80- or 90-mile trip from Nazareth to Bethlehem, where Mary and Joseph found a place to stay. Bethlehem was a peaceful town on a hill 6 miles south of Jerusalem. Probably only a few hundred people lived there at that time.*[4] Ask, *How long do you think it would have taken to travel from Nazareth to*

Bethlehem on foot? 3 or 4 days. *How long would it take us to travel that distance today by car?* Allow time for the children to make calculations.

Say, *Mary and Joseph stayed in a cave or stable with animals. It must have smelled like hay, barley, and oats that were in the mangers for the animals to eat. Mary laid Jesus in one of those mangers and swaddled him according to Jewish custom. Before a baby was swaddled, he was bathed in lukewarm water, then rubbed with salt, and then sprinkled with powder made from dry myrtle leaves. Then someone helped the mother hold the baby's feet and legs close to the body. The baby was placed on a square of cloth, his head in one corner and his feet in the other. Then the long, narrow swaddling band attached to the corner of the cloth was wound around the little body from the shoulders to the ankles to hold the "blanket" in place. The bands were 4-6" wide and 5-6 yards long. The mother wrapped the baby under his chin and also wrapped his forehead. Every day the baby was bathed again.*[5] Ask, *Would you like to swaddle a baby?* Allow the children to practice.

Say, *The first news of Jesus' birth probably was to shepherds. Why do you think this message was given first to shepherds? It was very dark in the hills where the shepherds were. A village off in the distance would not even appear very bright, because only the light of oil lamps would be burning there. The sight of the angels to the shepherds was very frightening. The Bible says the shepherds "came with haste," which may mean they jumped fences to see the child.* Turn out the lights in the room. Shine a flashlight on the ceiling as you talk about the angels. (See p. vii for another scene you might add to tell the shepherds' story.)

Ask, *If Jesus were born today, what would take the place of the cave? The donkey that carried them there? The bed for the baby?*

Display the printed statements concerning the birth of Jesus. Ask the children to retell the story by arranging them in the correct order.

Divide the children into 2 groups. Position them at opposite ends of the room. Sing in echo "Sing Hosannas" (see p. 172).

Say, *Jewish boys were dedicated to God 8 days after birth. When Jesus was small, Mary and Joseph took him to the Temple in Jerusalem 6 miles away to dedicate him. Then they offered a sacrifice. Do you think Mary and Joseph were rich or poor?* See Leviticus 12:6-8 and Luke 2:24.

Have the children face the large appliance box. Use it as a house. Outside the box, seat 3 men bearing gifts and dressed in costume. Let them sit while you tell this story:

Later, other visitors besides shepherds came to see Jesus, who was no longer a small baby. If you were going to see a newborn king, where is the first place you would go to find him? What about to the home of the present king? That's exactly what the wise men did. Herod's palace was inside the city walls. The wise men went to him there. They claimed to have followed a star to get there. These were real astronomers who studied the position of the stars and kept charts and records of their studies. But King Herod wasn't happy. He knew nothing about a newborn king. They probably didn't know it, but he was a very jealous man, so he sent them to Bethlehem to find out what they could.

The arrival of a caravan[6] *always brought the people to the city gate or well, particularly if the caravan came from a faraway place such as India or Persia, as this one did. The tinkling of the bells the camels wore could be heard above all the other sounds around the gate. While the camels were watered and fed, men listened to the stories of the travelers. By now,*

CELEBRATING

Bethlehem was buzzing with news of the new baby.

The wise men found the baby. They brought spices, frankincense, myrrh, and gold. The burning of spices was believed to heal and rid one's house of evil. Frankincense and myrrh were 2 of those spices. The wise men exit. *The young Jesus had at least two kinds of visitors —people considered very important and those considered very unimportant. Even in our time, all kinds of people can find Jesus and know him.*

Emphasize that Christmas is indeed a time of gift giving and memories. Hand out paper and pencil. Ask the children to complete this sentence: "Christmas makes me feel . . ."

Make a Christmas wreath: Cut out a large round green circle from posterboard. Cut out nonsecular pictures from old Christmas cards. Glue the pictures in collage fashion over the wreath circle. Cards can hang off around the edges. Glue a Christmas bow at the bottom. Hang the wreath where other groups can see it.

Make gift boxes: Write on slips of paper quotes from the Christmas story. Place these in small gift boxes or match boxes. Wrap boxes with Christmas wrap. Tie with ribbon. Ask each child to unwrap his/her gift and tell who made the statement and to whom it was said.

With adult supervision, make Christmas treats to give away. See (p. 91)

See (p. 91)

Lent

RESOURCES
appliance box
Bible headpieces
chalk or felt tip pens
chalk/markerboard
chart of Jesus' last week
"clubs"
copies of "The Trial"
costumes
"grave clothes"
highlighter marking pen
jars marked "myrrh" and "aloes"
Lord's Supper equipment
newspaper and magazine pictures of world leaders
oil
"palm branches"
paper
"spindle"
"swords"
table paper
"tomb"
tomb "stone"
water

PREPARATION
(may require several class sessions)

> Read again the information on "Celebrating Passover" (see p. 89). Review the events of that feast, especially what the people did at a Passover meal. It is of great importance in understanding Jesus' crucifixion.

> Secure costumes for Jesus, Pilate, the soldiers, the chief priests, the Sadducees, the High Priest, the Sanhedrin, the narrator, and the people.

> Borrow a spindle, which is a metal spike on a base used in offices for temporary filing of papers.

> Find newspaper and magazine pictures of present world leaders.

> Display Lord's Supper equipment.

> List on paper or chalk/markerboard the following events of Jesus' last week by days:

- Monday—drove moneychangers out of the Temple
- Tuesday—worshiped at the Temple
- Wednesday—unknown
- Thursday—celebrated Passover meal with disciples
- Friday—crucified on the cross
- Saturday—body in the tomb
- Sunday—arose from the dead

> Read John 18:28–19:16.

> Make copies of "The Trial"[7] (see pp. 98, 99). Highlight each character's part.

> Transform the room into an open area or find an appropriate outside area for dramatizing the trial.

> Use the large appliance box to represent the tomb. Place a round flat "stone" in front of the opening. In front of the tomb, display these items: large jars of spices marked "myrrh" and "aloes," grave clothes, oil, and water for washing the body (see pp. 19, 97 and John 19:39-42).

PROCEDURE

Dress several children in headpieces as soldiers, chief priests, and Sadducees. Attach swords to their belts, and have them carry clubs. Dress a child as Jesus, wearing a headpiece.

Assign the following roles in "The Trial" to different children: Jesus, Pilate, a Roman soldier, the High Priest, the Sanhedrin, the narrator, and the people. Dress the characters in appropriate costumes or just headpieces.

Position a Roman soldier on guard outside the door of the classroom before the children arrive. Give paper to the children and ask them to tear it up and throw it on the floor. Say, **Lent is a season many Christians observe to remember Jesus' life, death, and resurrection. It begins with Ash Wednesday in February and ends on** **Easter Sunday, a total of 46 days. We are going to talk about the last week in Jesus' life.** Ask the children to pick up the pieces of paper off the floor and place the pieces on the spindle. Say, **The world was trashed. It was sinful and displeasing to God. God said, "Why don't we make a collection place where all the pain and problems of the world can be stuck together?" Let's call that place "the cross." All the "junk" of the world was collected at the cross. Because of the death of Jesus, the world is a better place for us. Let's see how it happened.**

Show newspaper and magazine pictures of world leaders. Ask, **How did these people get to be leaders? Which of them are popular leaders? Which ones are not? Why was Jesus sometimes not a very popular leader?**

Ask, **What was the relationship of the Romans to the Jews at this time?** Talk about the Roman soldier stationed outside the door.

Say, **Jesus had warned his disciples that he was going to die, but they didn't want to believe him. For a long time Jesus had been making people angry. That doesn't mean he was wrong. It just means he made some people angry. They thought he would be the kind of king who would fight their enemies and deliver them from the Romans. Remember, they were captives of the Romans. But he wasn't that kind of a king. He had enemies who wanted to get rid of him.**

At the time of today's story, Jesus was going again to Jerusalem for the Feast of the Passover, as he had done for many years since he was a small child. This was to be his last time to attend the Feast. Two of his disciples found a donkey, and Jesus rode it through one of the big gates of the city. It was a special time. People who loved him cried out with joy.

Ask the children to make a long road from table paper. Place it on the floor. Scatter palm branches and several costumes along the road. Divide the children into 2 groups. Have them stand on either side of the room and pretend they are waving palm branches. Ask one group to say repeatedly, "Hosanna to the Son of David!" Ask the other group to say repeatedly, "Blessed is the one who comes in the name of the Lord." Say, *They were honoring Jesus as a king.* Ask, *Why did Jesus come to earth?* Say, *Pretend you see him coming. Greet him. Remember, it was a very happy time.*

Point to the chart listing the events of Jesus' last week by days. Say, *Let's talk about the last week of Jesus' life.*

On Monday, Jesus made a whip out of cords and drove some moneychangers out of the Temple. He said, "This is a place of prayer, but you've made it a den of robbers."

On Tuesday, Jesus returned to the Temple for his last day of work and worship there.

On Wednesday, we're not sure what happened. Perhaps Jesus visited with his friends Mary, Martha, and Lazarus in Bethany and also rested. He wanted to spend the last days of his life with people he loved.

On Thursday, Jesus celebrated the Passover meal with his disciples in an upper room. He washed their feet. This was usually done by a servant in a household. He said to his disciples, "Do you understand what I just did?" He helped them see that if he, the Lord and Leader, was willing to wait on them, they should be willing to serve one another. He did everything with them on that night that he had done at the Passover meals during his lifetime. Only this time, he was the lamb to be sacrificed. Because Jesus died on the cross as our sacrifice, we no longer kill animals as sacrifices for our sins. This meal was also called the "Last Supper."

Don't go into more detail than this—it is too symbolic for children to grasp. You have merely planted a seed for children to learn this concept when they are old enough to understand the statement "Here is the lamb of God who takes away the sin of the world." Ask, **What do we do in churches today to remember this important event?** Point to the Lord's Supper equipment.

Say, **Sometime during the meal Jesus said, "One of you will turn me over to my enemies very soon." Each disciple began to say, "Am I the one?" Jesus said, "It is 1 of the 12 who is dipping bread into the bowl with me." Judas knew it was he. And then Jesus talked to his disciples at the supper about his coming death. But still, no one wanted to believe he would die soon. Jesus and his disciples sang a hymn, as was the Jewish custom. About midnight Jesus led his disciples to the Garden of Gethsemane. Many olive trees grew there. In fact, the word Gethsemane means "olive presses." That very night Jesus was arrested. Judas came up to him with a crowd of Jesus' enemies. Judas had told them, "The man I kiss is the one you want."**

Ask the children dressed as soldiers, chief priests, and Sadducees to enter the room. Have them take Jesus out the door. Ask children in the large group to say things such as: "Hey you can't do that," "He hasn't done anything wrong," "You can't just walk in here and take someone, "What's he done to get arrested?" But the arrestors ignore them.

Say, **In that day and time, kissing someone meant you really loved them and you were the best of friends. Can you say that's true in this story? Was Judas the kind of person you'd expect a disciple to be? Would you want him for your best friend? Why did Judas have to identify Jesus anyway? Jesus had been in the Temple many times. Didn't his enemies know him already?**

CELEBRATING

Then another of Jesus' disciples betrayed him. Jesus had said to Peter, "Before the rooster crows, you will have denied 3 times that you even know me." Roosters crowed first about midnight. They crowed a second time about 3 A.M. They were so much on schedule with their crowing that Roman soldiers used it as a signal for the changing of the guard. Peter did exactly what Jesus said he would do: he denied he was one of Jesus' friends. When he heard the rooster crow, he remembered Jesus' warning. Tears ran down his face. He felt terrible about it. Jesus was badly mistreated, and then he was tried in a court.

In preparation for the trial, share the following information: *The Sanhedrin was a powerful group of men—priests, scribes, and religious leaders—who held court and settled arguments among the people. The Sanhedrin turned Jesus over to Pilate, who was the Roman governor and had been sent to Israel to make sure the people paid their taxes and behaved themselves.* Narrator and actors perform the play, "The Trial."

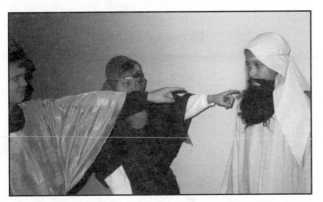

Jesus and His Accusers

Say, *On Friday, Jesus was crucified.* Ask, *What does the word "crucifixion" mean?* The act of nailing or fastening a person to a cross for the purpose of putting him to death. Crucifixion always took place outside the city walls. Say, *Once again, Jesus was away from home when an important event in his life happened. He was in Jerusalem at the time of his death. At*

sundown on the day of his crucifixion, the Jewish Sabbath began. No work was done from sundown Friday until sundown Saturday. Jesus' friends were sad, discouraged, and afraid.

On Saturday, Jesus' body was in the tomb,

On Sunday, Jesus rose from the dead. Have the children face the tomb. *Early on Sunday morning, women came to the tomb. Look in Luke 24:1-3 to find out what they were carrying in their hands as they came near Jesus' burial place. From what other Bible story do you remember the word "myrrh"? What was the women's shocking discovery when they arrived at the tomb?* Point to the display of spices.

Jesus' enemies tried to say he didn't rise from the dead, that his disciples just stole the body. Yet, 500 witnesses said they saw Jesus alive after the resurrection. Can you imagine 500 testimonies? How would that stand up in court? As you sit and look at the "tomb," can you believe that everything in this story really happened? That's what it means to be a follower of Jesus. Jesus made the world a better place. That's why we celebrate Easter!

CELEBRATING

The Trial

(based on John 18:28–19:16)

Narrator: Jesus' trial before Caiphas, the High Priest, ended in the early hours of Friday morning. Next, Jesus was taken to the palace of Pilate, the Roman governor. His accusers wouldn't go in themselves because it was against their Jewish rules, they said, and they wouldn't be allowed to eat the Passover lamb. So Pilate went outside to them.

Pilate: What is your charge against this man? What are you accusing him of doing?

High Priest and Sanhedrin: We wouldn't have arrested him if he weren't a criminal!

Pilate: Then take him away and judge him yourselves by your own laws.

High Priest and Sanhedrin: But we want him crucified, and we need your approval.

Narrator: This fulfilled what Jesus had said concerning the way he was to die. Then Pilate went back into the palace and called for Jesus to be brought to him. (Pilate turns around, moves back a short distance, and then faces Jesus.)

Pilate: Are you the king of the Jews?

Jesus: "King" as you use the word or as the Jews use it?

Pilate: Am I a Jew? Your own people and their chief priests brought you here. Why? What have you done?

Jesus: I am not an earthly king. If I were, my followers would have fought when I was arrested by the Jewish leaders. But my Kingdom is not of this world.

Pilate: But you are a king then?

Jesus: Yes, I was born for that purpose. And I came to bring truth to the world. All who love the truth are my followers.

Pilate: What is truth?

Narrator: (Pilate walks forward a few steps to his original place as Jesus steps aside.) Then Pilate went out again to the people and told them, "He is not guilty of any crime. But you have a custom of asking me to release someone from prison each year at Passover. So if you want me to, I'll release the 'King of the Jews.'"

Narrator: But the people screamed back,

People: No! Not this man, but release Barabbas!

Narrator: Barabbas was a robber. Then Pilate whipped Jesus' back with a leaded whip, and the soldiers made a crown of thorns and placed it on his head and robed him in purple. (A Roman soldier robes Jesus in purple, and places the crown on his head as Pilate looks on.)

Soldiers: Hail, "King of the Jews!"

Narrator: Then Pilate said to the Jews,

Pilate: I am going to give him to you now, but understand clearly that I find him "not guilty."

Narrator: Then Jesus came out wearing the crown of thorns and the robe. (Jesus walks forward.)

Pilate: See the man!

Narrator: At the sight of Jesus, the chief priests and Sanhedrin began yelling,

High Priest and Sanhedrin: By our laws he ought to die because he called himself the Son of God.

Narrator: When Pilate heard this, he was more frightened than ever. He took Jesus back into the palace again. (They retreat a few steps.) Pilate asked him,

Pilate: Where are you from?

Narrator: Jesus gave no answer.

Pilate: You won't talk to me? Don't you realize that I have the power to release you or to crucify you?

Jesus: You would have no power at all over me unless it were given to you from above. So those who brought me to you have the greater sin.

Narrator: Then Pilate tried to release him, but the Jewish leaders told him, "If you release this man, you are no friend of Caesar's. Anyone who declares himself a king is a rebel against Caesar." At these words, Pilate brought Jesus out to them again and sat down at the judgment bench on the stone-paved platform. (They step forward.) It was now about noon of the day before Passover. Pilate said to the Jews,

Pilate: Here is your king!

People: Away with him! Away with him! Crucify him!

Pilate: What? Crucify your king?

High Priest and Sanhedrin: We have no king but Caesar!

Narrator: Then Pilate gave Jesus to them to be crucified.

99

Notes

[1]Pilgrimage information adapted from Betty Goetz and Ruthe Bomberger, *Marketplace 29 A.D., A Bible Times Experience* (Stevensville MI: B. J. Goetz Publishing Co., 1989) 43, 140.

[2]Passover information adapted from *Jesus and His Times* (Pleasantville NY: Reader's Digest Assoc., 1987) 98, 99, 251-52.

[3]Adapted from Ceil and Moishe Rosen, *Christ in the Passover: Why Is This Night Different?* (Chicago: Moody Press, 1978) 52ff. Used by permission.

[4]*Wycliffe Bible Commentary*, Charles Pfeiffer and Everett Harrison, eds. (Chicago: Moody Press, 1962) 933.

[5]Adapted from Marion C. Armstrong, "Swaddling a Baby," *Home Life in Bible Times* (Nashville: Abingdon Press, 1943) 17.

[6]Ibid., "A Spice Caravan," *Life and Customs in Bible Times* (Nashville: Abingdon Press, 1943) 18.

[7]Original drama by Brad Kocher. Used by permission.

Chapter 10
SEARCHING: Having Fun with Research

Rationale

Someone has said, "Never provide for children information they can find for themselves." Sometimes you may ask the children to go to the Searching Stop and write down basic facts to report to a small or large group as the unit progresses. Answers don't need to be long and complicated; they can be short and abbreviated. You could tape some of the information the children need to know and keep the tape player in this area. Always have in the Stop the answers they are looking for. (See pp. 9, 10 for information on preparing the Searching Stop.)

Always give the children an opportunity to share with someone what they have learned. Otherwise, they will lose their motivation for inquiry. If necessary, supplement their information tactfully.

Give the children an occasional outside assignment, for example: bring a newspaper clipping about Jericho (if it is currently in the news), or watch a TV program that gives information on Jericho. You might also place in the Searching Stop clearly printed instructions of several things the children are to do. Encourage the children to bring information for the Searching Stop.

At times, as a result of a question that comes up during large group time, you may want to set up a small discussion group with several children. Let them go to the Searching Stop and find the answer or brainstorm an answer to it, reporting to the other children before they leave the session. Throughout a unit, leave in the Searching Stop words and definitions that apply to the unit.

Leader-Directed Research Activities

RESOURCES
Bible artifacts (replicas or pictures)
Bible story pictures
box
cassette recorder
cassette tape
colored paper
detective costume
newspaper clippings
pencils
plastic forks and spoons
resource book
sand

PREPARATION
> Write questions on different colored slips of paper. In a resource book on those pages where the answers to the questions are found, place matching colored strips of paper. Or, cut a piece of paper the color of the question and the size of the page of the book. Place the sheet in the book at the proper page. Cut the sheet so that it frames the answer on the page.

> Record on cassette tape a song or a small part of a Bible story.

> Put sand in a box. Hide replicas or pictures of ancient Bible artifacts in the sand. Make a diagram/answer sheet of where each item is located. Make up a worksheet, asking such questions as: Describe the article you found. What is its approximate age? By whom was it used?

PROCEDURE
Assist the children as they participate in the following activities:

- Study pictures of Bible stories. (See pp. 113, 114 for ideas on using pictures.)

- Choose a question strip, locate the matching color strip in the book, and find the answer to the question somewhere on that page.

- Listen to the taped song or Bible story to find a specific answer to a question and then report to the large group.

- Match Bible verses with pictures.

- Go on secret assignments. Dress as detectives, wearing glasses, big noses, hats, and badges.

- Go on a Bible dig. Use plastic forks and spoons. Complete the question sheet.

Individual or Group Research Activities

RESOURCES
bookmarks
carrots
empty container
paper
pencils
pitcher
reference books
salt
stepladder (4')
water

PREPARATION

> Display reference materials, Scripture verses, pictures, and other items in the Searching Stop.

> Write research questions on large sheets of paper. Display the papers in the hallway.

> On paper strips, write the names of different Bible characters[1] and Scripture references where their story is found. Place paper strips on a table in the Searching Stop.

> Place bookmarks at pages in reference books that tell about certain Bible character(s). Place the books on a table in the Searching Stop.

> Place on a table a pitcher of water, a box of salt, carrots, and an empty container.

> If possible, bring goats' milk for the children to taste.

PROCEDURE
Distribute the following assignments to individual children or groups of children:

- Using the reference books, write a short report about the Bible character whose name is on the table.

- Look up 1 Kings 17:1-7. What are ravens? Can you find a picture of ravens? What is a wadi?

- Find the meaning of the word "menorah." Why is it important to the Jewish people? Try to sketch on paper a menorah.

- Take the 4' stepladder into the hall. High on the wall you will see sheets of paper with questions on them. Carefully remove a question sheet. Bring it to the Searching Stop. Find the answer to the question.

- Choose a name from the table. Read the Bible story from the Scripture passage given. List on paper as many facts as you can about that person.

- Find an illustration of a plow pulled by oxen.

- Read Genesis 6:14-16. Determine the measurement of Noah's ark (a cubit is about 18"). To what could we compare the size of the ark today?

- Make a list of all the things sheep and goats were used for.

- Tell all you remember about Moses and his people crossing the Red Sea on dry ground. Now look up the story in Exodus 14:21-29 to see if your facts are correct.

- Choose a book off the table. Read the pages between the bookmarks. Draw a picture about what happened to the person in the passage. Share your picture with someone.

- Study about city walls and gates. Report on their significance.

- Find information on the Dead Sea. Learn why it is called the Dead Sea and why it is difficult to drown in this body of water. (The sea has a high concentration of salt, and the density [thickness] prevents swimmers from sinking.) Mix ½ cup water with ½ cup salt. Stir well. Drop in a small slice of carrot. Try to push the carrot down. What happens if you drop the carrot into clear water? The Dead Sea also has many minerals in it and tastes terrible! The beach looks like white sand, but the sand is actually salt. The Dead Sea is the lowest spot on earth. It is below sea level.

- Find where the Ark of the Covenant is now. Would you be excited if it were uncovered? Think about the importance of what was inside.

- Find out about Masada, a stronghold/fortress of the early Christians.

Leader-Directed Map Activities

RESOURCES
bedsheet
Bible pictures
cardboard
chalk
construction paper
crayons
felt tip pens
flour
foamboard
glue
iron
ironing board
maps (world and Bible lands)
newspapers
paints (acrylic/tempera)
paper squares (small)
particleboard
pencils
salt
sand
sponges
straight pins
string
table paper
teaspoon
window shade
yarn

PREPARATION
> Obtain/make copies of maps.

PROCEDURE
Assist the children as they participate in the following activities:

- Use crayons to draw a map of Palestine on an old bedsheet. Outline the countries in black. Use a different color of crayon for each province/area. Place another piece of cloth under the map. Place the map on an ironing board. Press the back with a hot iron so that crayon marks won't rub off.

- Use a mileage scale to measure distances on maps with string.

- To enlarge a map, use a pencil to divide the map into 1″ squares. If the map is to be 4 times as large, divide that paper into 4″ squares. In each large square, copy the lines exactly as they appear in the corresponding square on the small map. Write a small corresponding number in pencil in each square on both maps. Erase the numbers after you complete the map.

- Draw a permanent map of Palestine on a window shade (see pp. 110, 111). Add places to the map as needed. (Raise the shade when the map is not in use.)

- Circle places on the map as we name them during the story.

- Draw a large wall map on table paper. Draw on it or glue onto it small pictures of what happened at certain towns, for example, a paper fish where Jesus fed the 5,000, crutches where he healed someone, and a boat where he called James and John to follow him.

- Using chalk, draw a sidewalk or parking lot map of Palestine.

- Draw a map on table paper. Outline land and water areas with a felt tip pen. Then paint the areas. Add rivers, cities, and other features.

- Make a map using a piece of expanded foamboard measuring 36"x48"x½". You'll also need a teaspoon, pencils, felt tip markers, yarn, straight pins, water-based paints, and a world map or map of biblical lands. On the foamboard draw the world or an area you wish to portray. Mark the countries' boundary lines, rivers, oceans, and seas. Use the teaspoon to hollow out rivers, oceans, and seas. Color the water areas with blue markers. For the mountain ranges, cut triangular strips off the sides of the foamboard. Glue triangles on the board. Use different colors of paint to denote different types of land surfaces—brown for desert, green for grass, purple for mountains. Make small banner-style flags out of construction paper to mark what happened where.

- To make a relief map, use particleboard. You will also need a large table, a map to be traced, newspapers, water, and tempera paint. Build up land areas with papier-mâché (see recipe) or a salt and flour mixture (see recipe).

Papier-mâché

Tear newspaper into 1"x2" strips. Soak in water several hours. Tear the strips into smaller pieces. Squeeze out water. Mix a thick flour and water paste. Add newspaper pieces until the mixture is sticky. Apply the mixture to the base. Build up the surface for mountains. Indent it for valleys. Squeeze excess water from the mixture. Make a hole in it. Allow 1 or 2 days to dry. Paint the map with tempera, blue for water and tan for sand (or spread glue on the desert area and sprinkle sand on it). Dip bits of sponge in green paint to simulate trees. Identify locations on the map with tape and small paper squares.

Salt and Flour Mixture

Mix these ingredients: 4 c. flour, 1 c. salt, ½ c. water. Apply the mixture to a large piece of cardboard or other board, building it up for mountains and indenting it for valleys. Allow 1 or 2 days to dry. Paint with tempera, perhaps designating countries or areas with different colors. Identify locations with tape and small paper squares. (Use a map as a guide.)

Individual or Group Map Activities

RESOURCES

glue
maps
overhead projector
paints
paper
pencils
projector screen or blank wall space
table paper
transparencies
transparency markers
yarn

PREPARATION

> Make copies of "Palestine in Old Testament Times" (see p. 110).

> Make copies of "Palestine in New Testament Times" (see p. 112). Answers are given for leaders.

1. Nazareth
2. Bethany
3. Capernaum
4. Sea of Galilee
5. Bethlehem
6. Jerusalem
7. Jordan River
8. Jericho

PROCEDURE

Distribute the following assignments to individual children or groups of children:

- Pick up a copy of the worksheet "Palestine in Old Testament Times." Follow the directions. (See the "Joseph" map on p. 111 for help.)

- Pick up a copy of the worksheet "Palestine in New Testament Times." Follow the directions.

- Locate Midian. Write the name on a map. Find out what this land was like.

- Show travel routes of biblical characters. Glue colored yarn on the map or paint the routes in bright colors. Use different colors for trips to and from.

- Make a large floor map from doubled table paper. Draw Paul's journeys on it.

- Using transparency pens, draw maps on transparencies. Place the finished maps on the overhead projector. Project onto a screen or blank wall space. Use the pens to identify towns and countries and what happened in those places. Trace Paul's 1st, 2nd, and 3rd missionary journeys.

Sample Research Lessons

HOME LIFE IN NAZARETH

RESOURCES
Bible verses
bread
Jewish foods
olive oil
paper
pencils
raisins
reference books
small boxes (3"x5")

PREPARATION

> Assign foods to bring for a Jewish family meal.

PROCEDURE

Distribute the following assignments to individual children or groups of children:

- Tell about marriage customs of Jews in New Testament times.
- Find a picture of a typical house in Nazareth in New Testament times. Identify the furniture, tell what each item was used for, and compare the items to those in your house today.
- What is a mezuza?
- What was a typical day like in New Testament Nazareth? Who went to school? Who went to work? Who stayed home?
- Tell about Jewish mealtimes long ago.
- How did people bathe and wash their clothes in Nazareth during New Testament times?
- What did children do for entertainment during the time of Jesus?

Ask for the report on Jewish marriage customs in New Testament times. Supplement with this background information if needed:

Marriages were arranged by parents. Brides were usually only about 13 or 14 years old. Grooms were older. First the couple was betrothed. In the company of a priest and their parents the couple took an oath to love, honor, and be faithful to each other. They exchanged rings. *After that, it was sometimes a year before the wedding. During this time the bride lived with her parents. The wedding was at the home of the bride. There was singing, dancing, and eating for days or weeks.*[2] *After the wedding, the couple moved into their own home.*

Ask for the report on the typical house in Nazareth. Supplement with this background information if needed[3]:

Unless people were wealthy, they lived in a one-story house with one room. Everything was done in that room. Babies were born there; the family ate, slept, and worshiped there; and the children grew up and often married there. There were no beds, so the family members slept on woven mats. Each morning they rolled the mats up and put them in a corner or in a chest. The family sat on mats and cushions. A hollow place in the wall held clay water jars. A storage bin for grain was built into the walls. Goatskin water bags hung on the walls.

Houses were made of dried brick or rough stone. Attached to or underneath the house was a cave where the family animals were kept. There were no glass window panes, so the family used animal skins or heavy fabric to cover the windows. Most houses had dirt floors, so people used white sand to clean the floors, and then the dirt and sand were swept outside. The family members also cleaned their dishes with sand. Remember, water was very scarce. Washing and bathing were done outside so the dirt floors of the house would not turn into mud.

For light, the family used oil lamps (see p. 12). *These were small clay bowls. Owners filled them with olive or castor oil and floated wicks on the oil. They then lighted the wicks. Because there was little light, the family went to bed at dark and got up at sunrise.*

Jewish houses were flat-roofed. To make the roofs, branches were woven together and laid on top of rafters. Then the spaces between the branches were covered with a thick layer of clay, which formed a smooth, hard layer of plaster. After a rainstorm, a heavy roller was rolled over the roof. Each fall, a fresh coat of plaster was laid, and damaged sections were replaced. It was fairly easy to cut away and replace sections of the roof.

During the sunny part of the day, families dried olives and grapes on the roof. On warm nights, they took their sleeping mats on the roof and slept under the stars. The rooftop was also used for cooking, entertaining guests, or conducting family religious ceremonies. An upper room was constructed on the roof of some houses. Jesus and his disciples observed the Last Supper in a house with an upper room.

At Home in Nazareth

Ask for the report on a mezuza. Supplement with this background information if needed:

A mezuza is a small box about 3"x5" containing Old Testament verses. It was placed on the doorpost outside Jewish homes.

Ask for the report on a typical day in Nazareth. Supplement with this background information if needed:[4]

After a simple breakfast of olives, raisins, dates, and bread, the men started working in the fields. There they took care of their sheep and goats, planted seeds, worked on the plants, or harvested crops. They took cold bread, cheese, and fruit for their lunch, packed in a leather bag called a "scrip."

Women and young children walked through the narrow, winding streets, carrying water jugs to the town well. There the women exchanged news. Then the women and girls would take a donkey and gather fuel for the fire. The fuel was charcoal, thorn bushes, or dried grass. They ground their grain on a hand mill. The coarse flour was used to make bread. It was easier if 2 women could sit on the ground and work the mill together. Each held the handle on the millstone and turned it in a clockwise motion. The stones were about 18"-24" in diameter. The millstone looked like this.

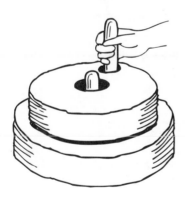

Millstone

Another chore of the women and girls was that of spinning wool into thread and weaving it to make clothing, blankets, and other items. During the day the boys went to synagogue school.

Ask for the report on Jewish mealtimes. Supplement with the following background information if needed:[5]

Mealtimes in Jewish homes were very different from ours. The largest meal of the day was served in the evening after sunset. A large cloth was spread on the floor. On top of it were placed trays of food and also bowls, cups, and other utensils. Family members sat on the floor or on low stools. The father blessed the meal.

People of Nazareth probably ate nuts such as pistachios and almonds, honey, cheese made from female sheep or goats' milk, beans, cucumbers, onions, lettuce, pomegranates, tomatoes, grapes, raisins, eggs, apples, garlic, butter, lettuce, peas, and parsley. Cut a pomegranate so the children can see the seeds. *They ate a lot of olives, both green and black ones. The olives were shaken off the trees with poles. Then they were placed in flat, round baskets that women carried on their heads. The oil was pressed out of the olives on an olive press. It looked like this.*

Olive press

The oil was used to treat wounds, to anoint royalty and the sick, to burn inside oil lamps, and to cook and season food. The olives were pickled in salt. Let children sample small pieces of bread dipped in olive oil.

Bread was the main part of a Jewish meal. The Jews did not use leavening, or yeast, to make bread rise, so most bread looked like thin, flat-shaped disks about 18" in diameter. Everyone broke off pieces of bread, dipped them into a rich stew, and ate with their hands. Most of the time the stew was made of lentils, beans, or vegetables cooked with sheep tail oil. The people ate little meat because a family's sheep and goats were needed for their wool, milk, and cheese. Sometimes, however, a piece of dove, pigeon, lamb, or fish was cooked in the stew. Occasionally, the family ate locust meat boiled in salty water. Sometimes they also ate dates, figs, melons, or some kind of berries or had a special dessert such as honey or thickened juice of grapes spread on bread or wheat cakes with honey. They drank water, wine, or milk from sheep or goats. Wine was diluted with water, sometimes 2 parts wine and 3 parts water, in order to weaken it and make it go further. Water was scarce and sometimes not drinkable. The alcohol purified the water. [6]

The Friday evening meal was the most special because the Sabbath was just beginning. A special lamp was lit, a special prayer was said, and the family listened to stories. Once a year, at Passover time, the family had a whole roasted lamb. If there was a family celebration for a wedding or naming a baby, the father might kill a sheep or a prized calf for the feast. You will recall that when the prodigal/ wasteful son came home, his father killed the fatted, or prized, calf.

People cooked on an open fire year-round. If the fire was inside the house, they built a pit of dried clay and stone. The smoke from the fire went out through the doors and window. Outside the people cooked on open fires or used ovens (see pp. 12, 108). *Outdoor ovens were built of clay, mud brick, or stone. Some ovens had 2 levels with 2 openings. A fire burned in the bottom level, and the food baked on the top level.*

Ask for the report on bathing and washing clothes. Supplement with this background information if needed: [6]

Water was very scarce, so people often used oil to clean their bodies. They rubbed their bodies with oil and dried them with a towel. Sometimes they used animal fat instead of oil because it was cheaper. The people used soap when there was water. They sometimes used ashes to clean their bodies. They also rubbed ashes on their clothing to get spots out. In some cities there was a common pool where the citizens went to wash their clothes.

Ask for the report on children's entertainment. Supplement with this background information if needed [7]:

For entertainment, girls played with dolls. Boys played a game similar to marbles, threw stones at targets, had slingshot practice, and performed tumbling acts. The children also played hopscotch and juggled. [8]

Ask, *Would you like to have lived in Nazareth during New Testament times? What would your chores have been? What would you have missed that you can do now? Would your life have been simpler? Do you think Jesus enjoyed growing up in Nazareth?*

Take the children outside. Play some of the games children of Nazareth played.

Ask the children to make a mezuza to place just outside the door of the classroom.

Eat Jewish foods at a family meal. As children enter the home for the meal, have them follow these Jewish customs: Remove shoes at the doorway. Wash hands and feet before eating.

SHIPS OF PAUL'S TIME

RESOURCES
pictures of ships
reference books

PREPARATION
> Print a list of questions for children to answer in groups.[8] For example,

- What risks would you be taking getting on a ship of Paul's time?
- Did the ships have compasses or sonar? How did they know where they were?
- How did the ships move from one place to another?
- Find the meaning of these terms: bow, stern, anchor, mainsail, topsail, cargo.

> Ask the children to bring pictures of ships from different time periods. Display these in the classroom.

PROCEDURE
Ask, *What do we want to learn about ships of Paul's time? How can we best organize to do that? What resources will we use?* Ask the children to choose from the list of research questions about ships. Ask them to prepare individual reports on ships of Paul's time, using brief, factual sentences. Ask them to compare their findings with the pictures of the ships on display.

Ask for the reports on ships of Paul's time. Supplement with this background information if needed[9]:

The ships of Paul's time were made of wood. The hull, or frame, was very strong and durable. Ships moved forward as the wind filled the large, square mainsails. But also, below deck and chained to benches, hundreds of slaves were forced to pull heavy oars in time to the beat of a drum. The oars steered the ships. Smaller sails aided in steering the vessels. Ships had pointed bows that could ram enemy ships. The ships boasted a long

spike that could be lowered onto an enemy boat, locking them together. The soldiers were then able to cross the bridge.

There were no passenger ships, just cargo ships. The ships carried items such as grain, wool, glassware, timber, wine, and olive oil from one port to another. They were steered by 2 side rudders (broad, flat, movable pieces of wood or metal for use in steering). The sailing season was late spring until early fall. In the winter the ships sat in harbors, waiting for good weather. There was no set schedule for travel because ships had to wait until the wind was right! Travelers spent many nights at different ports.

Notes

[1]A good resource is the *BibLearn Series on Biblical Personalities* (Nashville: Broadman Press).

[2]Adapted from Fred Wight, *Manners and Customs of Bible Lands* (Chicago: Moody Press, 1953) 124ff.

[3]Information on houses adapted from *Jesus and His Times* (Pleasantville NY: Reader's Digest Assoc., 1987) 93-94.

[4]Adapted from Wight, 80-90.

[5]Adapted from "Foods of New Testament Times," in *Exploring 2 Kit for Leaders* (Nashville: The Sunday School Board of the Southern Baptist Convention, August 1990); and John D. Davis, *Dictionary of the Bible* (Philadelphia: Westminster Press, 1929) 820.

[6]Adapted from Wight, 84-85.

[7]Adapted from *Faith for Life Curriculum* (Pittsburgh: Logos System Assoc., 1989).

[8]Group investigation method adapted from Bruce Joyce and Marsha Weil, *Models of Teaching* (Needham MA: Allyn & Bacon, 1986) 219-24.

[9]Adapted from *Jesus and His Times*, 182-83; and Chris Tarrant, *Life in Bible Times* (Nashville: Abingdon Press, 1985) 44-45. Used by permission of Scripture Union.

SEARCHING

Palestine in Old Testament Times

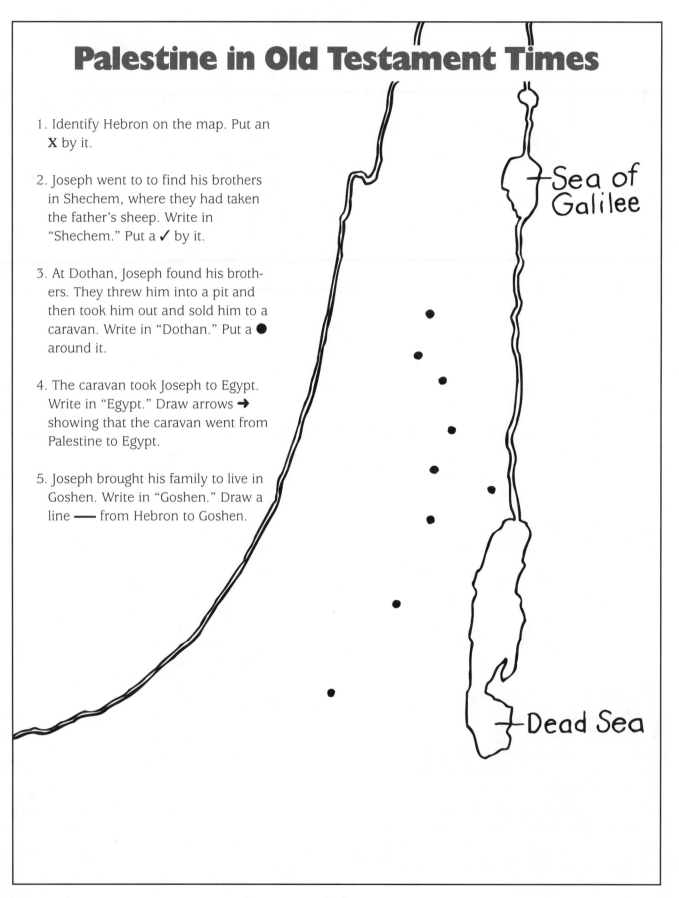

1. Identify Hebron on the map. Put an **X** by it.

2. Joseph went to to find his brothers in Shechem, where they had taken the father's sheep. Write in "Shechem." Put a ✓ by it.

3. At Dothan, Joseph found his brothers. They threw him into a pit and then took him out and sold him to a caravan. Write in "Dothan." Put a ● around it.

4. The caravan took Joseph to Egypt. Write in "Egypt." Draw arrows ➔ showing that the caravan went from Palestine to Egypt.

5. Joseph brought his family to live in Goshen. Write in "Goshen." Draw a line — from Hebron to Goshen.

Sea of Galilee

Dead Sea

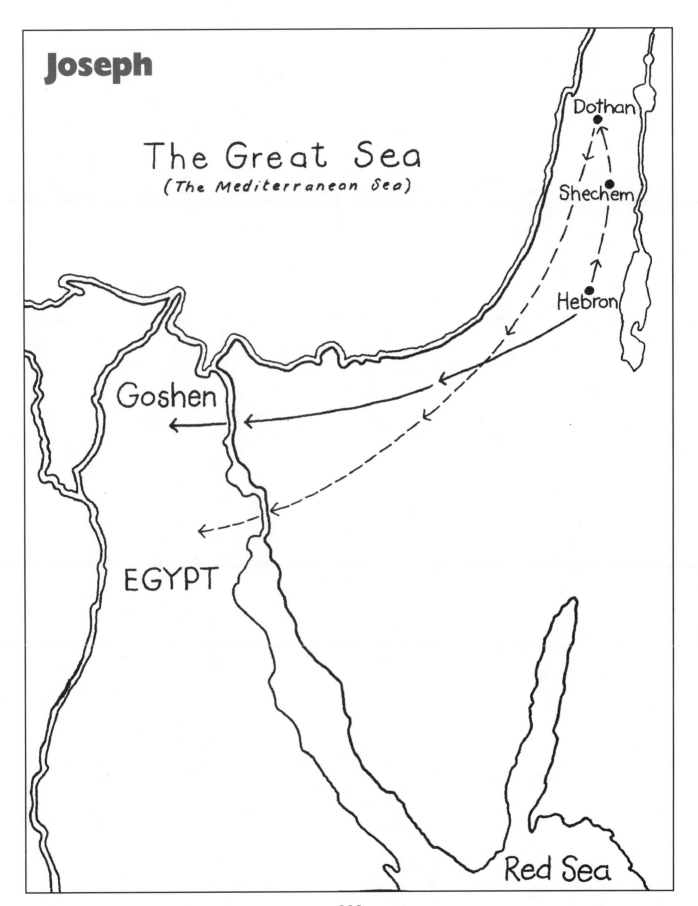

Joseph

The Great Sea
(The Mediterranean Sea)

Dothan

Shechem

Hebron

Goshen

EGYPT

Red Sea

Palestine in New Testament Times

Fill in the blanks with the name of the correct biblical place. Choose answers from the list at the bottom of the page. Draw the item named in each statement beside the correct location.

1. Jesus grew up in _____ and lived until there until he was 30 years old. Draw a small boy.

2. Jesus had special friends in _____ and often ate with them. Draw a small loaf of bread.

3. Jesus often visited in _____ near the Sea of Galilee. Draw a small boat.

4. Jesus loved the _____. Once he stopped a storm there. Draw a small fish.

5. Jesus was born in _____. Draw a cave or manger.

6. Jesus went to _____ often. He was killed there and rose again to life. Draw a temple.

7. Jesus was baptized in the _____. Draw stick figures of John the Baptist and Jesus.

8. In _____, a man climbed a tree to see Jesus. Then Jesus went home with him to eat. Draw a tree.

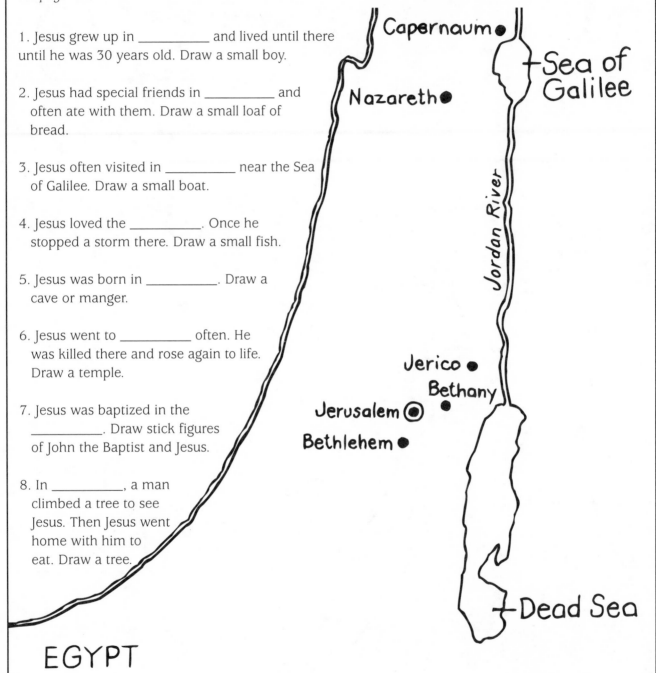

Answers: Bethany, Bethlehem, Capernaum, Jericho, Jerusalem, Jordan River, Nazareth, Sea of Galilee

Chapter 11
IMAGING: Using Visuals to Stimulate Thinking

Rationale

As children use visuals, Bible stories come alive for them. Instead of just imagining what it was like, they're able to transport themselves back into biblical lands. They're able to visualize the layout of the land, the people, and the animals. They can actually sample the foods. They can participate in the religious, educational, and social lives of the people.

Children remember much more of what they see, touch, taste, and smell than what they hear. By working with visuals, facts they never considered emerge. Drawing pictures helps them learn about shapes, sizes, textures, and distances. Their minds are stretched as new images are presented. Scenes and incidents take shape and form.

In this chapter are numerous ideas for making different visuals and for using them to enhance Bible teaching. Also included are suggestions for more effective use of commercially prepared materials.

Leader-Directed Imaging Activities

RESOURCES
appliance box
encyclopedia
fig bars
figs
grapes
honey
map
pictures (sets/individual characters/themes)
raisins
reference books
roast lamb
rope
unleavened bread
yardstick

PREPARATION
> Prepare unleavened bread and roast lamb.

> String fresh figs on a thin piece of rope. Hang to dry.

PROCEDURE
Use these activities with most stories:

• Show a group of pictures on the same subject. Ask what each picture in the group has in common with the others.

• Cover a large picture. Uncover it for 15 seconds. Ask the children to look at it. Cover it again. Ask the children to tell what they saw.

• Instead of telling a story, show an illustration of it. Ask enough questions so that the children will eventually tell the entire story themselves. Then review it.

• Show a picture of _____. Say, *Heroes are never afraid. What about the person pictured here? Do you know his/her story?*

Use these activities with specific stories:

- Study carefully a picture of the Passover feast. Pass around samples of unleavened bread and roast lamb.

- When you talk about John the Baptist, provide samples of bread with honey.

- Ask the children where they might find fresh figs. Show the string of dried figs. Tell the children that in biblical times figs were pressed into cakes, eaten fresh or dried, or applied to the body as medicine. Provide fig bar samples.

- Ask the children to dry some grapes at home in the sun. Ask later, *Did they turn into raisins? Did you have a flat roof on your house to put them on as the people of Israel did?* Or, make a simulated New Testament house from a large appliance box. Construct steps going up the side of the house. Place grapes on the roof. Pretend several days have gone by. Replace the grapes with raisins to show how they dried in New Testament times. Pass around samples of raisins. Ask, *Where in your country would you find flat roofs?*

- Show a picture of Nehemiah building the wall. Send several children to the Searching Stop to discover how thick the wall was. Offer assistance for converting measurements into feet. Use a yardstick to measure that distance out from the wall of your room to show how thick the wall was.

- Show a picture of Goliath. Read 1 Samuel 17:4. Send a child to the Searching Stop to find out how long a cubit and a span are. Ask for the report. (A cubit is about 18″, or the distance from the elbow to the tip of the middle finger. A span is a little more than 8″, or the distance between the end of the thumb and the little finger when the hand is spread.[1] Calculate Goliath's height. Mark it on the wall of your room.

- Show a picture of Daniel. Ask, *How did Daniel feel when he stood before the king? Can you hear his knees knocking? Can you hear his heart beating? Have you ever had to have great courage to do something?*

- Show a picture of the prodigal son. Ask, *Do you think he was homesick? How did he get back home? What did he say to his father? For what purpose did he leave home?*

- Show a picture of Saul on the road to Damascus. Ask, *How long do you think it took Saul to make the journey from Jerusalem to Damascus?* Look together at a map to see the distance. Ask the children to describe the scenery along the way. Find "Damascus" in an encyclopedia. Show the children a description of Straight Street, which still exists today. Ask, *What was the importance of this street in Saul's story?*

- Show a picture of Jesus feeding the 5,000. Ask, *Where might the disciples have gotten the baskets for the leftovers? What would 1 boy be doing with 5 loaves and 2 fish? Do you suppose that was lunch for his whole family?* Poor people ate bread made from barley, and wealthy people ate bread made from wheat. *What does this tell us about the boy?*

- Show a picture of life in Nazareth. Ask, *What could you learn about Nazareth from this picture? Would it be a pleasant place to spend a weekend? To live?*

- Show a picture of a well. Ask, *What was so important about going to the town well? How many wells did a town usually have? Why do you think the women looked forward to going to the well? Weren't the water jars heavy to carry—not to mention the leather buckets the women had to carry for getting the water from the well? What would be the fun of carrying a heavy water jar back and forth to the town well? What were the men and boys doing while the women and girls did the household chores?* (see p. 107)

Individual or Group Imaging Activities

RESOURCES

acetate paper
black construction paper
cardboard
china marking pen
easel
erasable marking board
glue
newsprint
paper
pencils
posterboard
pictures (Bible and modern-day)

PREPARATION

> Collect appropriate picture(s) for each activity. Place in appropriate locations.

> Glue pictures on cardboard. Cut into puzzle pieces.

> Write on posterboard cards descriptions of Bible characters.

> Cover cardboard with acetate paper (available at a leader's supply store). Or, obtain an erasable marking board.

> Cut footprints from black construction paper.

> Make copies of "What Do You See?" (see p. 122).

PROCEDURE

Distribute the following assignments to individual children or groups of children:

• Study carefully the picture on the easel at the room's entrance. Write a short paragraph about it.

• Study carefully the scene in the picture. Write an account of it as if you had witnessed the scene.

• Sketch from memory a _____. Then ask the leader to show you an actual picture of what you have drawn to see how well you remembered the details.

• Look at the large group of pictures. Set aside only those that go with our story for today (or the unit).

• Fit together the pieces of the picture puzzle to identify the story.

• Match the pictures of Bible characters with their proper description cards.

• Make a list of questions about the picture(s) to ask the other children.

• On the erasable board, write in cartoon-style what the characters are saying to each other.

• Glue illustrations onto newsprint in proper sequence to tell the story.

• Follow the large, black, paper footprints on the floor. Stop wherever you see pictures on the floor. Answer your list of questions by looking at the pictures.

• Write a script of the conversation you think is taking place in the picture.

• Look on the floor at pictures of Jesus preaching, teaching, and healing. Write on paper the characteristics of Jesus as shown in the pictures.

• Bring modern-day pictures that you can compare to biblical stories. For example, compare pictures of famous trials with Jesus' trial. Then make a poster of the pictures.

• Look in today's Bible passage. What images does the writer of this story "draw" with her words? (examples: green grass, blue skies, etc.)

• Study the picture of _____ carefully. Then complete the worksheet "What Do You See?"

IMAGING

Making Original Pictures

RESOURCES

chalk
cardboard tubing from clothes hangers
Christmas cards
cloth scraps
construction paper
corks
cotton swabs and balls
crayons
felt tip pens
glue
hairspray
hay
newspaper
onions
paintbrushes
paper towels
pencils
posterboard
potatoes
Q-tips
sawdust
soft drink cartons or muffin tins
sponges
spray bottle
sticks (small)
straight pins
straw
string
table paper
tempera paints (dry/liquid)
toothbrushes

PREPARATION

> Choose a location close to a sink if possible.

> Spread a thick pad of newspaper on a table. Keep plenty of paper towels handy.

> Double table paper.

> Place jars of tempera paint in a soft drink carton for easy transport. Or, pour paint into muffin tins.

> Have paintbrushes avaiable. (Cosmetic, vegetable, and pastry brushes make great paintbrushes.)

PROCEDURE

Assist children in making the following images:

- *Dry tempera painting*: Dip a cotton ball into the paint. Rub it on the picture. Use cotton swabs for small detail. Use colored chalk to draw the lines. Set the picture with a spray of water or hair spray applied from a distance.

- *3-D effect*: Glue pieces of sponge to the backs of cutouts. Glue cutouts to paper.

- *Tear-picture*: Tear objects out of colored construction paper. Glue the objects onto a large piece of paper.

- *Stencil effect*: Use straight pins to attach shapes to paper. Use a spray bottle to paint the sheet. Allow time to dry. Remove the shapes. Or, use a muffin tin with a different color paint in each section. Paint with sponges, Q-tips, corks, potatoes, onions, string, and toothbrushes.

- *Pictionary*: Instead of giving a written description, define words by drawing or glueing on pictures and writing simple definitions by each.

• *Clothing*: Cut out cloth scraps. Glue scraps onto the people in a scene. Use rough cloth for shepherds and farmers, and rich brocades and silks for wealthy people.

• *Nature scenes*: Use straw for hay, cotton for clouds and sheep, sawdust for camel's hair, and green-colored sawdust for grass.

• *Trees*: Dip small sticks in glue and then in shredded green paper. Or use orange, red, and yellow shredded paper for the leaves of a fall scene. For palm trees, make the trunks out of cardboard tubing from clothes hangers. Cut branches out of green construction paper. Stuff into the cardboard tube.

• *Storm at sea*: Use crayons to draw a violent, stormy sea. Glue on stand-up whitecaps.

• *Christmas cards*: Cut out scenes from old Christmas cards. Make new cards. Or, make a giant-sized card to display outside the room at Christmas.

Using Films, Filmstrips, and Videos

RESOURCES
A-V equipment
bleach
chalk
chalk/markerboard
felt tip pens
filmstrip (old or blank)
flashlights
map
microphone (pretend)
paper
paper lunch bags
pen for filmstrip
pencils
popcorn (and popper or microwave)
tape

PREPARATION
*Always preview visuals before showing them to children.

> Compile a list of terms/definitions used.

> Locate on a map the region(s) discussed.

> Compile a list of comments made.

> Compile a list of facts about the information conveyed through the visual.

> Study the Bible story passage carefully.

> Obtain an object related to the visual.

> Write questions concerning the visual. Tape questions under the chairs.

> Purchase blank filmstrips. Or, bleach an old filmstrip with Purex. Rinse well, or use soapy water to get the bleach off. Dry. Place a good filmstrip beside the old one. Mark off the frames with a special pen used with filmstrips.

PROCEDURE
Before Viewing:

• Distribute the word lists.
• Ask the children to note how the words are used.
• Distribute the comments list.
• Ask the children to record who makes each comment and in what situation.
• Appoint teams to listen for certain facts.
• Distribute the facts sheets.
• Guide in a study of the Bible story. Ask the children to look for things in the visual account that are also mentioned in the Bible account of it, and also to note what is missing in either account.
• Ask the children to watch for certain objects and to observe them closely.
• Ask the children to observe specific features such as clothing, houses, and villages.
• Assign ushers with flashlights to seat the viewers in a dark room. Serve popcorn in lunch bags.

IMAGING

During Viewing:

- Stop the visual at critical points and ask the children what they think will happen next. Then continue showing it.

After Viewing:

- Assist the children in locating on a map the region(s) discussed.
- Discuss the list of comments.
- Using a pretend microphone, interview the children concerning their opinions of the presentation.
- List events in the visual on the chalk/marker board or paper.
- Ask the children to put the events in the correct order.
- Ask for reports from the fact-finding teams.
- Discuss the differences and likenesses between the biblical and visual accounts of the story.
- Ask the children to write a critic's review of the visual
- Display an object related to the visual (example: an alabaster jar).
- Ask what the object had to do with the story.
- Ask the children to sketch from memory the objects they saw.
- Ask the children to quote some Bible verses they heard.
- Ask the children to describe certain features in the visual.
- Instruct the children to find and answer the questions taped under their chairs.
- Ask the children to pretend they are actors in the visual and write about what happened.
- Ask the children to list on paper each of the characters in the visual and then write some words to describe each of them.
- Ask the children to fill in each frame on the blank filmstrip and make their own filmstrips to share with the group later.

Sample Imaging Lessons

THE LAME MAN

RESOURCES
picture of lame man
sandals
sleeping mat

PREPARATION
> Place a sleeping mat and 2 empty sandals on the floor.

PROCEDURE
Ask the leaders and children to sit around the mat and sandals. Ask the children to open their Bibles to Mark 2:1-12. Show a large teaching picture of the story. Ask a child to summarize the story in 3 or 4 sentences. Encourage discussion by asking questions:

In what town did this happen? Do the people look happy? What sounds would you hear if the scene came to life? What do you think the sick man is saying to Jesus? What were the roofs of houses like? See p. 106. *Luke 5:19 gives us a clue. Look it up. What is the owner of the house thinking about the big hole? Who paid for the damages to the roof? What if it were raining?*

Describe the bed. Look up Matthew 9:2, Mark 2:4, and Luke 5:18. What is the bed called in each of these Scriptures? Why did it take 4 people to let the man down through the roof? What would have happened if 3 men had carried him? How do we know he didn't weigh 300 pounds and that's why it took 4 men to help him? Look at the size of the ropes. Is that a clue as to how heavy the man and the bed were? Is it summer or winter? In which season would the man have been heavier? Do you think this was the bed the man slept on all the time? What do you think he did with it after the healing experience? Look up Luke 5:24. What did Jesus say to do with the bed?

Do you think the lame man was wearing sandals when he entered the house? Wouldn't he need them when he left? Where did he get the sandals to walk after Jesus healed him, or did that make any difference? Do you think that perhaps this was the first pair of sandals he ever had? Can you imagine his joy at being able to walk away in sandals as other people did, or being able to walk at all?

Look through the Bible passage. Is there anything else you would draw into the picture? Who in this story dared to criticize Jesus? In what way? If you had just been healed, would it bother you to hear someone criticizing? Are the sandals the most important part of this story? If not, what is? Look at your own shoes. Do they make you feel lucky?

GALILEAN FISHERMEN

RESOURCES
cord
garden netting or fishnet twine
picture of Galilean fishermen
scissors
weights

PREPARATION
> Make a fishnet. Knot together squares of twine. Or, buy netting at a garden shop or a fishnet at a military surplus store. Cut the netting in a round circle 5'-6' across. Attach weights all around the top so the net will sink. Attach some long cord in a way that will help you draw the net closed by pulling the cord.

PROCEDURE
Ask the children to stand and position themselves so as to form the shape of a fishing boat and also to imagine they are fishermen. Ask, **Do you feel the sea spray in your face? Do you smell the fish? Pretend a terrible storm comes up. What will happen to us?** Sway from side to side. Pantomime the action. Explain that there were often bad storms on the Sea of Galilee.

Show a picture of Galilean fishermen. Spread out a fishnet. Ask several children to help you hold it. Say, *As we hold this, can you imagine Galilean fishermen, such as James and John, fishing with nets? The Bible talks about casting the nets. The net sunk to the bottom, and the fishermen cautiously tightened the rope and pulled in the net so the fish could not escape. Wasn't that good thinking? Imagine the net being full of fish. Would you be strong enough to pull it in?*

Jesus' disciples were not weak men. They were big, strong, and hardworking. Sometimes they cast nets from their boats. They not only had to keep the nets working well, but they also had to keep their boats in good shape. Often the nets were so full of fish, they broke and had to be mended. Jesus called some men to be his disciples while they were mending their nets. Do you remember who they were? What does mending mean?

What else would you need to take in the boat besides nets? Who would be there? Who often sailed in these boats that you might like to have on board as a special guest?

Let's plan a time when we can go to a pond, lake, or swimming pool and take turns "casting the net" to see if we can do it as well as Jesus' disciples did.

PHYLACTERIES

RESOURCES
black paint
match boxes
paintbrushes
picture of phylactery
ribbon

PREPARATION
> Review information on phylacteries.

> Try to arrange a trip to a Bar Mitzvah.

PROCEDURE

Show a picture of a phylactery. Say, *When a Jewish boy became 13 years old, he was considered old and wise enough to know the Law. The day a Jewish boy became Bar Mitzvahed was one of the most wonderful days of his life. Now he could wear a phylactery on his left arm. A phylactery was a little black leather box that had a tiny V-shaped sign in a raised letter on top. Inside were verses from the Law written on tiny scrolls of parchment. Straps were attached to the box. The straps were wrapped around a boy's arm in a special way 7 times. He would also wear a phylactery on his forehead, with the straps wrapped around his head with the ends hanging over his shoulders. When the boy took the phylacteries off, they were kept in a small bag.*[2]

Make phylacteries from small, empty match boxes. Paint the boxes black. Allow to dry. Place Scripture verses inside. Attach long ribbons to the boxes. Ask the children to wear the phylacteries on their arms and heads.

Attend a Bar Mitzvah.

ISRAELITES MAKING BRICKS

RESOURCES
dirt
molds
old shirts
picture of Israelites making bricks
straw
water

PREPARATION
> Arrange for a place to make bricks.

> Obtain necessary supplies.

PROCEDURE
Show a picture of the Israelites making bricks in Egypt. Tell the children that they, too, will make bricks. Dress them in old shirts. Mix 3 parts soil and 1 part straw. Add enough water to make the mixture like clay (fairly thick). Mix well. Pack into molds. Dry in the sun.

Ask, *How long did it take you to make one brick? Imagine making thousands of them. Once Pharaoh got angry with the Israelites. He said he would no longer furnish straw for them, so they would have to find their own, but they would have to make just as many bricks as usual.* See Exodus 5:7-8. *Don't you think that was pretty unreasonable? That's one of the reasons why the Israelites didn't want to be slaves any longer. They prayed that God would send someone to rescue them. Did God send someone? What was the rescuer's name?*

CHARIOTS

RESOURCES
2 chairs of same height
picture of Philip and the eunuch in a chariot
posterboard

PREPARATION
> Review information on chariots.

> Obtain necessary supplies.

PROCEDURE
Show a picture of Philip and the eunuch in a chariot. Say, *Chariots usually were made of wood or metal. Horses pulled them. There was a built-in case for carrying weapons. These cases were especially helpful for soldiers in wartime. The Israelites didn't use chariots too much for fighting because the land was too hilly. Remember when the chariots of Pharaoh's army sank in the Red Sea while chasing Moses and the people of Israel?* See Exodus 15:4-5. *What all could you do with a chariot? What did Philip use it for?*

Make a chariot. Place 2 chairs of the same height side by side. Make 2 large wheels out of posterboard, or use tires already in the room. Attach 1 wheel to each side of the chariot.

NEW TESTAMENT LETTERS

RESOURCES

boiler
hot plate or microwave
paper
paper grocery bags
pencil
picture of Paul writing a letter
tea bags
waxed paper

PREPARATION

> Print a passage out of one of Paul's New Testament letters to churches.

> Boil 1 cup water and 11 tea bags. Steep 10 minutes.

PROCEDURE

Show a picture of Paul writing a letter to a church. Show the Bible passage to the children. Explain the importance of letter writing in the early days of Christianity. Ask the children to make a letter like one Paul might have written. Say, *Tear a large piece of paper out of a large grocery bag. Scallop it around the edge with your fingers. Dip just the edges of the paper into the tea solution. Take the paper out. Dry it on waxed paper. Write the Bible passage on it. Display your letter somewhere in the room.*

Notes

[1]Adapted from Betty Goetz and Ruthe Bomberger, *Marketplace, 29 A.D., A Bible Times Experience* (Stevensville MI: B. J. Goetz Publishing Co., 1989) 78.

[2]Adapted from *Jesus and His Times* (Pleasantville NY: Reader's Digest Assoc., 1987) 150.

IMAGING

What Do You See?

Answer each question based on the picture you just saw.

1. What would you fail to see if you didn't look closely at the picture?

2. What things in the picture are not mentioned in the Bible?

3. Look at the expressions on the faces of the people.
   Who is happy, sad, angry, frightened? What is each person probably thinking?

4. Do the people look as if they have just been through a bad experience?
   What common feelings has this group just shared?

5. Imagine you are someone in the picture. What are the things you might enjoy
   seeing, tasting, touching, hearing, and smelling?

6. Was the artist true to the Bible in painting _____'s face?

7. In what ways does the artist make us aware of the time of day?

8. What do you think happened after the event in this picture?

Chapter 12
INTRODUCING/REVIEWING: Beginning/Reinforcing a Unit of Study

Rationale

How can you give children a favorable reception into a new year of Bible study? A social event before the first session of the new year is helpful for the leaders and children to get acquainted. It is a time for leaders to consider the needs of the children as individuals and as a group and also a time for bonding.

A new unit of study means a new adventure with your class. Before it begins, you might mail simple assignments to the children that they will complete and share with the group on the first Sunday of the new study. Most curriculum materials are taught in units of study, so it's important to make proper introductions.

As a child, did you enjoy memorizing Bible verses by repeating the selection mechanically? Probably not. There may be more fun ways to learn verses related to your units of study. For example, hearing verses read several times or reading verses repeatedly to oneself are great learning methods. Whatever the method, make sure the children have an understanding of verses they learn.

Review of a unit of study is just as important as the introductory or teaching activities. Review can make the study an unforgettable experience and helps to separate it in the minds of the children from a new unit approaching. Of course, review also provides reinforcement of stories.

Various games, both competitive and non-competitive, are excellent means of review. Determine what you wish to accomplish with each game, whether it be for fun only or for learning facts simultaneously. To avoid embarrassment for children who may not know the answers, allow team answers. Encourage players not to give yes and no answers. If they don't answer right away, give them time to think.

This chapter is about getting started—starting a new year, beginning a new unit of study, learning new verses—and about reinforcing what the children have learned. Included are suggested activities for providing meaningful new and review experiences for the children in your class.

Introductory Activities

A NEW YEAR

RESOURCES
construction paper
felt tip pens
glue
index cards (3"x5")
magazines
newspapers
paper
paper bags
pencils
yarn

PREPARATION
> Cut pieces of paper into 2 puzzle pieces. Write on the pieces these instructions: (1) Find the person with the puzzle piece that fits yours. (2) Find out 1 interesting thing about the person and share it with the rest of the group.

> Using 1 index card per person, write in scrambled form the names of the children and the leaders. If there are duplicate first names, add the first letter of the last name. Attach yarn to each corner of the card.

PROCEDURE

Use the following activities separately or in any combination:

- Divide the children into small groups. Offer a large selection of magazines and newspapers. Ask the children to tear out pictures of actions that describe themselves and things they like to eat, read, play, and so on. Have them glue these pictures onto sheets of paper. Let them introduce themselves by showing these pictures in the large group time.

- Distribute paper and pencils. Ask the children to write their names on the top of a sheet of paper and then drop the sheet into a paper bag. Instruct the children to pull out another child's name from the bag and then to write on the paper positive things about the child whose name is on the sheet. Read these aloud.

- Distribute construction paper. Say, **_From this piece of paper, you are to tear out the shape of something you're especially interested in or involved in, for example, dolls, clothing, baseball, or the piano or another musical instrument. Let the others in the room guess what the object is. Then tell us why you are so interested in this._**

- Distribute index cards. Ask the children to write something about themselves that no one else in the room knows. Collect the cards, mix them up, and redistribute them. Ask the children to read the message and guess whose card they have.

- Hand a puzzle piece to each child. Give a signal to begin the information search. Ask the children to share their findings with the group.

- Ask the children and leaders to find their name cards, unscramble the letters, write their names correctly at the bottom of the cards, and wear them around their necks as nametags. Have everyone wear these for several Sundays until the children and leaders are well-acquainted.

A NEW UNIT

RESOURCES
blindfold
books
boxes
bulletin board border and decorations
chalk
chalk/markerboard
curriculum leaflets
fabric remnants
felt tip pens
filmstrip
glue
index cards (3"x5")
magazines
magnifying glass
newspapers
paper (various types)
paper bags (large/small)
pencils
pens
posterboard
pushpins
scissors
string
tablecloth
tape
teaching pictures

PREPARATION

> Prepare a bulletin board or portable board with the new unit emphasis. Cover the background with giftwrap paper, table paper, or freezer paper. If you use flowered paper, fasten silk flowers or butterflies at the corners. Use the same colors as those in the paper. Use pushpins to attach placards, Bible verses, illustrations, a songsheet, even an actual item—for instance, a boat, a paper scroll, and written descriptions from the Bible. For variety, use pinking shears to cut around sheets of paper you plan to use. Place a border—either bought, homemade, or hand-drawn—around the board. For backgrounds, you also could use inexpensive items such as newspaper, leftover fabric, or sections from large grocery bags.

> Make a display of the unit subject. Use boxes and books to form different levels on a table. Cover with a cloth. Put into the display items that relate to the subject. Make stand-up labels out of posterboard to identify items. For example, for a unit on worship, show types of churches through the ages, such as an altar, a tabernacle, a temple, a store front building, an African hut.

> Make a poster with a question/statement regarding the unit. Print in very small letters so that it can be read only with a magnifying glass. With a string, attach a magnifying glass to the poster. Place it outside your room. (Hint: Print the message while looking through the magnifying glass. Use a very sharp pen or pencil).

> Using different sizes and types of print, make title posters or banners. For variety, print titles on giftwrap paper or wallpaper or on a seasonal-type item. For instance, during a March study, write the unit title on a kite, and hang it from the ceiling.

> Write on index cards words the group will study in the unit.

> Use a large duplicate picture relating to the subject or Bible characters. On the back, draw lines to divide it into puzzle pieces. Cut the picture apart.

> Write unit questions on paper or sentence strip board.

> Use 3 small paper lunch bags. On the outside of one print "Facts," on another "Places," and on another "Verses." On slips of paper, print under each category some things the group will study.

PROCEDURE
Use the following activities separately or in any combination:

• Show word cards to the children. Do not give the meaning of the words. Later in the unit, show the words again and ask for definitions.

• Ask the children to put the picture puzzle together to figure out what the new study is.

• Ask the children to listen for a particular word you will use a lot during the large group time. Say the word repeatedly throughout your conversation. Ask the children to guess the mystery word and what they think it has to do with the new study.

• Ask the children to take off their shoes and pile them in the center of the room. Blindfold a child. Ask her to use her sense of touch to find her own shoes and put them on. If she puts on someone else's shoes, say, *There's an old Indian saying that goes like this: "Never judge a man until you've walked a mile in his moccasins." Walking in someone else's shoes—that's what we'll be doing all year. We'll find out some ways biblical people were just like us but also different. During this unit of study we'll talk about the following people, and we'll "walk in their shoes."* List these characters on paper or chalk/marker board.

• Read unit questions before and after presenting the Bible story for each session.

• Tell the children to pay close attention to the unit filmstrip they will see. After the viewing, ask them to sketch from memory some things they saw, for example, how the clothing and houses looked.

• Place on the floor all teaching pictures for the new unit. Ask the children to arrange them in the order in which the events happened.

• Ask each child to select a piece of paper containing a fact, place, or verse; read it aloud; and then put it into the proper bag.

• Distribute children's leaflets from the printed curriculum. Let the children compete to see who will be first to find such items as the unit title, a puzzle

INTRO/REVIEW

or game they could do, a special Bible verse to learn, a story about someone, and an illustration.

- To introduce a study on God's world, take the children on a scavenger hunt outside the building. Distribute paper grocery bags. Ask the children to collect litter, trash, and other items they find. When they return to the classroom, ask them to make a montage (a picture in which objects are collected and can be superimposed, each on top of the other) by gluing onto paper the junk they collected. They can add tape, string, and other things to make the montage interesting. Leave the montage on display throughout the study.

NEW MEMORY VERSES

RESOURCES
beanbag
Bibles (several versions)
chalk
chalk/markerboard
construction or other colored paper
envelopes
felt tip pens
index cards (3"x5")
paper
plastic bottle
ribbon

PREPARATION
> Print each word of a verse on a separate piece of paper. Make a set for each child. Place the papers in envelopes.

> Use 2 sheets of colored construction paper. Print a verse on 1 of the sheets. Cut out key words from the verse. Place a sheet of another color under the paper on which the verse is written. Print the missing words so they fit the cutout spaces. Repeat this for other verses. Group verse cards together, and key word cards together.

> Write a verse in scrambled form on paper.

> Write each word of a verse on an index card. Make 2 sets of the words.

> Print only the consonants of a verse on a chalk/markerboard or paper.

> Write on paper significant verses found in the unit. Roll the paper like scrolls. Tie with ribbon.

PROCEDURE
Use the following activities separately or in any combination:

- Ask families to choose a verse that is associated with the study. Urge them to say the verse together before each meal of the week. Ask them to choose another verse at the end of the week. By the end of the year, each family will have learned 52 verses.

- Distribute the filled envelopes. Ask the children to dump the contents of their envelopes onto the floor and put the words in proper order. Ask several children what their verses say. They'll discover they all have the same verse. Repeat the verse together several times.

- Ask the children to match the key word and verse card sheets and to tell in their own words what the verses mean.

- Ask the children to unscramble the verse. Then hand out several versions of the Bible. Ask different children to read the verse aloud from each translation. Decide together which translation you unscrambled.

- With the children seated in a circle, play the game of "gossip" using a Bible verse. Start the verse from each end of the circle by whispering it in someone's ear. Ask each child to pass it around the circle by quoting it to the next child. When the verse meets in the circle, see if it sounds the same. Make necessary corrections. Repeat it together several times.

- Turn each word card face down. Ask each child to turn up 2 cards. If the cards match, the children may remove the words. In order to familiarize the children with the words of the verse, play until all

INTRO/REVIEW

the words are taken out. Then rearrange the words in the correct order and read them aloud.

- Read a verse aloud. Say, ***Write a word or words you heard.*** Read the verse again. Say, ***Write more words you heard.*** Continue the process. Say, ***The words don't have to be in order. You don't have to make a sentence with them. Just get the words in your mind.*** When you think the children are ready, ask them to put the words together to form a verse.

- Ask the children to sit in a circle. Toss a beanbag around to each child. As the children catch it, they must give 1 word from the verse and then toss it back to the leader. Continue playing until all children can say the verse together.

- Display the consonants of a verse. Ask the children to add the vowels.

- Ask the children to sit in a circle. Spin a plastic bottle. When the bottle stops, read half of a verse to the child the bottle is pointing to. Ask the child to quote the other half of the verse. Give points for each verse correctly quoted. If someone cannot complete the verse correctly, ask another child to quote it. Award the points to that child.

- Each Sunday, hand a scroll to a different child. Ask that child to teach the verse to the large group during that session.

Review Activities

RESOURCES
beanbag
board games
cassette player
cassette tape
chalk
chalk/markerboard
children's leaflets
felt tip pens
index cards (3"x5"/5"x8")
masking tape
overhead projector
paper
paper brads
pencils
pictures related to studies
posterboard (different colors)
rubber washer
scissors
spinner from board game
straws
toy cars or animals
transparencies
yarn

PREPARATION

> Prepare review questions for each game.

> Place a small, round rubber washer under a game spinner attached to cardboard. Fasten securely on the back side of the cardboard with a large paper brad.

> *Beanbag Toss:* Divide a posterboard into 5 sections. Number each section (1, 2, 3, 4, 5).

> *What Does It Mean?:* On the left side of a posterboard write several words to be defined. Beside each word, place a paper brad with a piece of yarn wrapped around it. On the right side of the board, list short definitions in random order. Place a paper brad beside each word on the posterboard.

> *Color Wheel*: Using 2 colors of posterboard, cut 2 large circles. Make 9 smaller circles of each color.

> *Getting There*: Write 1 review question from the unit on each 3"x5" card. Draw 1½"x1½" squares around the edges of the posterboard. Print "Start" on a square and "Finish" on another. Print names of places on several board squares named in the unit. On the back of each 3"x5" card, give a number value (1–4). You may design some hazard cards also (examples: flat tire, sick donkey, go back to _____).

> *Whirling Windows*: Cut 2 large circles of posterboard, with 1 smaller than the other. Cut 1 window out of the smaller circle. Draw windows around the edges of the larger circle. Place a review question in each window. Place the smaller circle on top of the larger circle. Fasten them together with a small rubber washer and a paper brad.

> *Where Am I?*: Write riddles to answer the question.

> *Jeopardy*: Divide a posterboard into equal sections. On each section, write an answer based on a particular scripture passage.

> *Who Am I?*: On index cards print names of Bible characters in the study.

> *Pick-Up Straws*: Print a list of review questions. Number the questions. Number drinking straws to correspond to the numbers of the questions.

> *I'm on My Way*: Set up an overhead projector and a transparency map.

> *Hide-and-Seek*: Hide printed review questions around the room.

> *What's My Line?*: On strips of paper print words that different Bible characters in the unit study said.

> *What's Important?*: On index cards write words or phrases from the study.

> *Fill in the Blanks*: Write a review of the study, leaving some blanks to be filled in. Make copies.

> *Great Is the Lord*: Write a speech chorus based on the study. Make copies for the children.

> *Who's Who?*: On index cards write clues about Bible characters in the study.

> *True or False*: On slips of paper write the names of different Bible characters in the study.

> *Memory Match*: On slips of paper write scripture references used in the unit.

PROCEDURE

Use the following activities separately or in any combination:

- *Beanbag Toss*: Ask the children to take turns throwing a beanbag into one of the 5 sections on the board. Ask a review question to each child. Children who answer their question correctly will receive the number of points they landed on.

- *What Does It Mean?*: Instruct the children to stretch the pieces of yarn beside the words on the posterboard to the answers that match the words.

- *Color Wheel*: Divide the children into 2 teams. Assign team colors. Line up 9 pictures from the study. Place 3 pictures in each row. In turn, the teams choose a picture and tell a fact about it. If the fact is correct, they may place a team-color circle on the picture. The first team to have a complete line of circles either horizontally, vertically, or diagonally wins the game.

- *Getting There*: Allow children to choose tiny toy cars or animals for markers. Place the stack of question cards upside down on the gameboard. Ask each child to choose a card. If he answers the question correctly, he moves the number of spaces printed on the back of the card. If he answers incorrectly, he must put the card on the bottom of the stack. The first child to reach "Finish" wins the game.

- *Whirling Windows*: In turn, the children will spin the top circle, making sure they land over a window. They read aloud the question in the window and try to answer it. If the answer is correct, they receive 10 points.

- *Where Am I?*: Read riddles to help children answer the question "Where am I?" For example, "I am riding in a chariot and reading from a scroll. Where am I?" or "My shepherd friends and I have come to see the baby. Where am I?"

- *Jeopardy*: Assign a Scripture passage for children to read. Ask them to choose an answer from the board and then to supply the question that goes with the answer.

- *Silent Movies*: Ask several children to pose silent scenes of stories from the unit. Ask the rest of the group to identify the story.

- *Who Am I?*: Tape a card onto the back of each child. Each child will turn her back to the others. The group gives clues until the child guesses who she represents.

- *Pick-Up Straws*: In turn, the children throw the pile of straws down and then try to pick up 1 straw without moving the others. If they move a straw, even the slightest bit, they lose their turn. If they succeed, they answer the corresponding question for points.

- *Bible Bee*: The children will answer review questions in spelling bee fashion. As long as they answer questions correctly, they can continue to stand. If they miss the answer to a question, they must sit down. The last child standing is the winner.

- *What Do You Think?*: Ask questions such as: What do you remember most about what we studied? What was the most fun? Did you find out anything that surprised you? What was a new thought for you?

- *I'm on My Way*: Using an overhead projector, project a transparency map onto the wall. Trace the journey of a Bible character (example: Paul's or Moses' journey).

- *Hide-and-Seek*: Ask the children to find the review questions and answer them.

- *What's My Line?*: As you show each phrase, ask the children to identify the person who made the statement and his reason for saying it.

- *What's Important?*: Ask the children to explain the significance of the words or phrases to the study.

- *Stump the Staff*: If you are teaching in a church or school setting, invite some of the staff members in to answer review questions. Ask them to review the stories before they come to your room.

- *Fill in the Blanks*: Distribute copies of the story you wrote. Ask the children to fill in the blanks either with words or illustrations.

- *What a Character!*: Choose a Bible character from the study. Ask the children to help present a character analysis of the person. Ask questions such as: Was she kind? Was he selfish? Was she devoted to God? List the traits on paper or chalk/marker board.

- *Echo Psalm*: Choose a psalm on the subject you studied, one that repeats lines. Choose several children to go into another part of the room and play the part of an echo.

- *Great Is the Lord*: Assign parts in the speech chorus for high voices and low voices. Ask the readers to present it orally. End with the group saying in unison, "Great is the Lord and greatly to be praised."

- *Who's Who?*: Read or show the clues on the cards. Ask the children to identify the persons.

- *What If?*: Ask a startling question related to a Bible story. For instance: What if someone gave you a million dollars? Let the child who responds tell the story.

- *Man/Woman of the Year*: Ask the children to think about the characters in the study. Ask who they would choose for "Man/Woman of the Year" and why. Ask if anyone would like to challenge the nomination. Discuss the reasons. Ask for other suggestions.

- *Design a Game*: Ask the children as individuals or groups to design their own games using their own questions, posterboard, children's leaflets, and felt tip pens. Instruct them to direct play of the games.

- *Something New*: Ask individual children or groups of children to record on cassette tape new thoughts they had from the unit. Play the tape for the large group.

- *True or False*: Seat several children in a circle. Give each child in the circle a paper with the name of a different Bible character in the unit and a 3"x5" card. Ask these children to write 2 true facts about each Bible character and 1 false statement. Collect the cards and then redistribute them within the circle. Children in the circle are to guess which character is represented on the card and which fact is false.

- *Memory Match*: Distribute scripture references used in the unit. Allow children 30 seconds to look up the verses in their Bibles. Then ask them to close their Bibles and write on paper as much of the verse as they remember.

Chapter 13
RESTING: Learning Without Supervision

Rationale

The best way to avoid discipline problems is to engage children in activities from the minute they enter the classroom. Because the Rest Stop requires no adult assistance, it can be used when leadership is limited or with early arrivers, children who finish an activity before the others, or disruptive children in a small group who need to be separated from the others for a short time. The activities can be done by the children at any time during the unit—to preview a new study, to learn facts in the current study, or just for fun.

The Rest Stop requires some pre-session work from the leaders but is well worth the effort. Plan 5 or 6 activities for each unit. Include activities that appeal to a wide range of senses and types of learners. Prepare all activities before the 1st session of a new study. Attach printed instructions for each task on a pattern cutting board or on a piece of cardboard covered with table paper or acetate paper. Lean the board against the wall. You may wish to record the instructions on a cassette tape as well.

Suggestions for activities are included in this chapter and grouped according to subject matter. The basic ideas can be easily adapted for other units of study. (See chapter 10 for directions on setting up a Rest Stop.)

Experiencing God

RESOURCES
Bible
cassette player
cassette tape
china marking pen
instruction board
lapboard
paper (table and acetate)
pencils

PREPARATION

> Make copies of "My Feelings About God" (see p. 136). Place them on the floor.

> Make copies of "Scrambled Verse" (see p. 136). Place them on the floor. See John 4:24 for the answer.

> Write on the board: Find on the floor the worksheet "My Feelings About God." Follow the directions. When you finish, discuss your answers with a leader.

> Write on the board: Print on a sheet of paper the word "GOD." On the same sheet, write graffiti (lettering and drawings) about God, for example, Great, Totally Awesome, Always There, Knows Everything. Express your true feelings about God.

> Write on the board: Find on the floor the worksheet "Scrambled Verse." Follow the directions. When you finish, check the Bible to see how well you did.

Jonah

RESOURCES

Bible
cassette player
cassette tape
china marking pen
instruction board
lapboard
paper
pencils
picture of Jonah

PREPARATION

> Make copies of "Complete-a-Sentence" (see p. 137). Place them on the floor.

> Write on the board: Find on the floor the picture of Jonah. On a piece of paper, write what is happening in the picture.

> Write on the board: Find on the floor the worksheet "Complete-a-Sentence." Look up Jonah 1:1-3 in your Bible. Follow the directions for completing each sentence.

Christmas

RESOURCES

board for instructions
cassette player
cassette tape
colored dot stickers (removable)
china marking pen
musical score of a children's Christmas song
paper
pencils
piano or keyboard
posterboard

PREPARATION

> Cut 13 small bells and 1 large bell from posterboard. Print each name on a small bell: Joseph, John the Baptist, Saul of Tarsus, Jesse, David, Micah, Isaiah, Zacharias, Moses, Elizabeth, Mary, Matthew, Timothy.

> Choose a children's Christmas song (non-secular). Attach a colored dot below each word on the songsheet and to the corresponding note for each word on a piano/keyboard. Place the song on the floor.

> Make copies of "Check Your Facts" (see p. 137). Place them on the floor. Answers and references are given for leaders.

1. (C) Matthew 2:1)
2. (I) (Matthew 2:1)
3. (G) (Matthew 2:4)
4. (A) (Micah 5:2)
5. (B) (Matthew 2:8)
6. (D) (Matthew 2:9)
7. (E) (Matthew 2:10, 11)
8. (H) (Matthew 2:11)
9. (F) (Matthew 2:12)

> Write these instructions on the large bell, and then attach them to the board: Which people did God use to work out His plan for sending Jesus? Take a sheet of paper from the floor. Look through the small bells on the floor. Choose at least 5 persons who answer the question. Write their names on the piece of paper.

> Write on the board: Find a copy of a Christmas song on the floor. Take it to the piano/keyboard. Under each word of the song you will see a colored dot. Play the note on the piano/keyboard that has the same-colored dot. Continue to the end of the song.

> Write on the board: Find on the floor the worksheet "Check Your Facts." Follow the directions. Check your answers with a leader.

RESTING

Helping at Home

RESOURCES

Bible
cassette player
cassette tape
children's songbook
construction paper
envelope
china marking pen
instruction board
paper
pencils

PREPARATION

> Cut the shape of a house from construction paper.

> Draw a simple house floor plan. Make copies. Place the copies on the floor.

> Choose a children's song on the subject of helping at home. Record the music and words on cassette tape.

> Print on a strip of paper a Bible verse on the subject of home or family. Print some of the key words on small pieces of paper. Cut them out and place in an envelope. Blacken the key words on the verse strip.

> Write these instructions on the paper house, and then attach them to the board: Look on the floor. Choose a house floor plan. Write in each room things you could do to help in that room at home. (Example, prepare a meal in the kitchen.)

> Write on the board: Listen to the song on tape. Make up several questions you could ask your friends. Rewind the tape when you finish so another child can do the activity.

> Write on the board: Find an envelope and a Bible verse strip on the floor. Fill in the blackened spaces on the verse strip with the words found in the envelope. Then read all of the verse to yourself.

Daniel

RESOURCES

Bible
bookmark
cassette player
cassette tape
china marking pen
glue
instruction board
magazines
paper
paper towels
pencils
plastic bags
vegetable samples

PREPARATION

> On the floor place magazines, pieces of blank paper, and plastic bags filled with vegetable samples.

> Make copies of "Match-Up" (see p. 138). Place them on the floor. Answers: 1-G; 2-F; 3-E; 4-C; 5-B; 6-E; 7-D.

> Write on the board: Pick up a piece of plain paper off the floor. Find pictures in the magazines of the kinds of food and drink Daniel and his friends asked for. Glue them onto the piece of paper. Write at the top of your sheet "Food for Daniel and His Friends." Eat samples of the vegetables you will find in the plastic bags. Tell what the vegetables are.

> Write on the board: Pick up the Bible on the floor. Turn to Daniel 1, the section where the bookmark is located. Read the quotes below. In the blank following each quote, write the name of the person who said the words.

• "The king has decided what you are to eat and drink, and if you don't look as fit as the other young men, he may kill me." _____(Ashpenaz)

133

• "Test us for 10 days. Give us vegetables to eat and water to drink. Then compare us with the young men who are eating the food of the royal court. Then base your decision on how we look."
_____(Daniel)

> Write on the board: Find on the floor the worksheet "Match-up." Follow the directions.

Creation

RESOURCES
cardboard
cassette player
cassette tape
china marking pen
construction paper
felt tip pen
glue
instruction board
nature slides or nature video
paper
pencils
slide projector or VCR/TV
table paper or newsprint

PREPARATION
> Cut a piece of cardboard 10½"x10½". Cover it with table paper, newsprint, or another white paper. Print at the top "Creation." Cut a 4"x5" pocket from construction paper. Glue the pocket onto the right side of the cardboard. On the left side print the following instructions:

1. Take a card from the pocket (limit of 5 cards).
2. Read the description.
3. Write on the card the name of something God made that fits the description. Then write 2 words that describe that object.
4. Then write at the bottom of the card, "Thank you, God, for _____."

Cut cards small enough to fit into the pocket. Write on each card 1 of the following phrases:

• something green that stands tall
• something with feathers
• something that can fly
• something that has a skeleton
• something with scales
• something fuzzy
• something curved and colorful
• something blue
• something with big teeth

> Make a tape with words and music to the song "This Is My Father's World." Take the tape and a tape player to the Music Stop.

> Write on the board: Take a piece of paper and a pencil. Go to the Music Stop. Listen to the tape of "This is My Father's World." Write all the things you heard in the song that God made. Share your findings with a friend.

> Make copies of "What People Can Do" (see p. 138). Place them on the floor. Answers: yes-1, 3, 4, 5, 7, 8, 11/God

> Write on the board: Find on the floor the worksheet "What People Can Do." Follow the directions.

> Place on the floor a slide projector/VCR and TV containing slides/video of nature scenes.

> Write on the board: Ask a leader to show you how to operate the slide projector/VCR and TV. Look at the slides/video about God's world. How many things do you recognize?

RESTING

Moses

RESOURCES

Bible
Bible dictionary
cassette player
cassette tape
cloth scraps
filmstrip or video
filmstrip projector or VCR and TV
glue
instruction board
paper
pencils
posterboard
resource book
scissors

PREPARATION

> On the floor place a filmstrip projector/VCR and TV containing a filmstrip/video about Moses.

> Cut paper dolls from posterboard. Cut scraps of cloth. Place on the floor.

> Write on the board: Find the word "manna" in a Bible dictionary. Tell a friend what manna is. See if both of you can remember what you've learned without writing it down.

> Write on the board: Open your Bible to Exodus 17:1-7. Read the story about Moses and water from the rock. Make up 3 questions about the story. Write them on a piece of paper. Ask the questions to a friend in the room to see if she knows the answers.

> Write on the board: Watch the filmstrip/video. Turn it off. On a sheet of paper write 3 things you remember about Moses. Share your answers with a leader.

> Write on the board: Find paper dolls and a small pile of cloth scraps on the floor. Design and cut costumes from the cloth scraps for the following people: Moses, Pharaoh, the princess, Aaron, the priest. (See pp. 31-33) Glue the costumes on the paper dolls.

Saul

RESOURCES

Bible
cassette player
cassette tape
envelope
felt tip pen
instruction board
paper
paper grocery bags
pencils
ribbon

PREPARATION

> Enlarge the worksheet "Word Trips" (see p. 139). Cut at the dotted line. Cut out the word pictures from the story of Saul's conversion (Acts 9:1-9). Place the word pictures in an envelope.

> Place on the floor pieces (larger than letter size) of brown paper bags torn roughly around the edges.

> Write on the board: Find on the floor the worksheet "Word Trips" and the envelope of shapes. Match them. The words are in order according to the events of the story. Use the words to tell someone in the room the story of Saul's conversion experience in Acts 9.

> Write on the board: Look up Acts 9:10-19 in your Bible. As you read the story of Ananias and Saul, think of a Bible verse that speaks about friends. Did Ananias show that he might have known that verse as he dealt with Saul?

> Write on the board: Find part of a brown paper bag on the floor. On it write a letter that Saul might have written to Ananias, thanking Ananias for restoring his sight. Roll the letter into a scroll. Tie it with ribbon. On the outside, under the ribbon, place a small piece of paper addressed to Ananias wherever you think he might be at the time. Also plan how you will get the letter to him.

RESTING

My Feelings About God

Write "T" for true statements. Write "F" for false statements:

___God will give me anything I ask for.

___There are some reasons why I should be afraid of God.

___God is like a parent.

___God has strict rules for us to follow.

___God will punish us if we disobey God's rules.

___God's people are always happy.

___God knows everything I'm thinking.

___God is everywhere at the same time.

....

Scrambled Verse

Unscramble the verse. Write it correctly at the bottom of the page.

"dog is tirips nda setho isphwor mih sumt isphorw imh ni itirps nad rutht." (John 4:24)

Complete-a-Sentence

Complete this sentence as you think Jonah would have completed it before he got on a boat to go to Tarshish: I don't have to do what God says, so I'll _____.

Complete this sentence as you think Jonah would have said it after arriving at Nineveh: I made a mistake. When God gave me a command, I should have _____.

Complete this sentence as you feel it should be completed if God gives you a command: If God tells me to do something important, I will _____.

Check Your Facts

Choose an answer from the list at the bottom to fill in the blank.

1. _____ was the king of Judea when Jesus was born.
2. Who came from the East to find the child Jesus? _____
3. Herod asked the _____ and _____ where the child was born.
4. In what town did the prophet Micah say that Jesus would be born? _____
5. What did Herod tell the wise men? _____
6. The _____ guided the wise men to the child Jesus.
7. The wise men were filled with great _____ when the star stood over the _____ where Jesus lived.
8. The wise men gave thanks to God for Jesus by _____ and _____.
9. How did God warn the wise men not to return to Herod? _____

Facts

A. Bethlehem
B. search diligently and tell him where the child was found
C. Herod
D. star
E. joy, house
F. in a dream
G. chief priests, scribes
H. worshiping, giving gifts
I. wise men

Match-Up

Draw a line from the name or place in the 1st column to the words in the 2nd column that identify the person or place.

1. Nebuchadnezzar   A. put Daniel in the lion's den

2. Shadrach, Meshack, Abednego   B. King Nebuchadnezzar's chief official

3. Cyrus   C. blazing furnace

4. A place of punishment   D. another name for Daniel

5. Asphenaz   E. King of Persia

6. King Darius   F. Daniel's friends

7. Beltshazzar   G. King of Babylon

What People Can Do

Place a check in the box beside those things people can do.

❏ Take care of pets
❏ Put together a universe and make it operate
❏ Learn how weather works and how to predict future weather
❏ Explore space
❏ Make new laws about how people should act toward one another
❏ Keep the earth moving so that seasons will change
❏ Discover new materials to keep people warm in winter and cool in summer
❏ Replace some worn-out parts in the human body
❏ Make a human body
❏ Cause rain to fall
❏ Discover the proper medicine to cure a disease

Who gave people the ability to do the things you checked?

WORD TRIPS

- THREATS
- SYNAGOGUES
- FLASHED
- PERSECUTE
- SPEECHLESS
- EYES
- THREE

Chapter 14
PRAISING: Worshiping Through Music and Prayer

Rationale

Music was an important part of Jewish life in biblical times. The people sang at special celebrations, when traveling together, on feast days, when they harvested crops, at weddings, at dedications, at coronations, and at every major victory. Often the singing was actually chanting from the book of Psalms.

The Jewish people also played various instruments:

- trumpets
- double-reed pipes
- timbrels
- cymbals
- sistrums
- lyres
- harps
- tambourines
- flutes
- castanets
- drums

Some of these instruments undoubtedly came to the Israelites from the Egyptians.

The Jewish people played trumpets in the Temple when the burnt offering was laid on the altar and also when the gates of the city closed at night. Trumpets were first made from the horn of an ox or ram and were about 18" long. Next came curved metallic trumpets, and then straight trumpets.

Lonely shepherds played and sang as they took care of their sheep. They probably made double-reed pipes by cutting small holes out of reed-stalks.

Timbrels were like today's tambourines. They looked like hoops made of brass or wood. Skin from sheep or goats was drawn tightly around them. Small bells hung around the edges.

Cymbals looked much as they do today.

Sistrums were metal rattles or noisemakers. They had a thin, lyre-shaped metal frame, through which passed a number of loosely-held metal rods.

Music was important to the Hebrews in their worship. Children need to learn about various aspects of worship. Use the Music Stop often. If you teach where there are no hymnals, written music for children, or musical instruments for accompaniment, record songs you wish to sing, or buy accompaniment tapes. Plan music activities that are meaningful and related to the study or that are intended for a certain purpose. When considering the use of a particular song, ask yourself:

- What is the purpose for using the song?
- Is the song singable for the particular age group?
- Is the song easy to learn by repetition?
- Are the words and music well-matched?
- Is the range of the music appropriate for the children's voices?
- Does the song include symbolic language children cannot relate to?
- Are the meanings of all the words clear to the children?
- Is the melody singable, likable, and easy to hear?
- Does the song relate to the present study?
- Does the song say something important?
- Is the accompaniment simple?
- Does the rhythm of the notes match the speech patterns?
- Is the text of the song long and wordy or short and simple?
- Is it a melody you can hum as you work or play?
- Does the song express a familiar concept, or does it teach a new idea?

Prayer is also a form of praise and worship. The Bible speaks often of prayer. We can pray in private or public, either alone or with others. Children need to learn to talk to God spontaneously. As they grow in their ability to recognize problems and needs, and to learn and understand about God, the more they will respond to God. They will also learn to pray for others and will feel more comfortable when others pray for them. In teaching children about prayer, consider the following suggestions:

- Be flexible with prayer time rather than limiting it to an opening prayer or a dismissal prayer. Occasionally, interrupt the study to lead or ask someone else to lead in prayer.
- Discuss with the children the best positions for praying—kneeling, standing, or other.
- Encourage the children to name the people they know who are praying for them.
- Urge the children to keep small prayer notebooks and to write in them the names of people they want to pray for on different days of the week, and then to continue to add names to it.
- Help children deal with unanswered prayer or with grief by saying, "Why don't we ask for what we want to happen? If it does happen, we will be so happy. If not, let's ask God to help us while we cry." Or, "I don't know why this happened, but I'm so glad I can cry with God and to God about it."

Included in this chapter are activities that will help children experience music and prayer as worship.

Music Activities

RESOURCES

aluminum pie plates
Bible
cake pans (9″ square metal)
cassette player
cassette tapes
coffee cans
construction paper
cord
dowel sticks (1/2″)
dried beans
felt tip pens
fringe
glue
gold bells (12 mm./metal)
greeting card boxes
hymnbooks
leather scraps
magazines
metal pot lids
musical instruments
musical selections
newspapers
oatmeal boxes
paint
paper
pencils
"plumber's elbow" (plastic)
posterboard
ribbon
rubberbands
sandpaper
stapler
staples
table paper
toothpicks
window shade
wooden blocks

PREPARATION

> Cut dowel sticks to the desired length.

> Prepare a sign that reads: "Listen. What are these songs about? They are clues to what we might talk about."

> Cut out pictures from magazines and newspapers that illustrate some of the words or phrases of a certain song.

PRAISING

> Print the words of a song on a large sheet of paper. Leave out words for which children can substitute a picture.

> Print Psalm 150 on table paper as follows:

All: Praise the Lord!
Girls: Praise God in his sanctuary;
Boys: Praise him in his mighty firmament!
Girls: Praise him for his mighty deeds;
Boys: Praise him according to his surpassing greatness!
Girls: Praise him with trumpet sound;
Boys: Praise him with lute and harp!
Girls: Praise him with tambourine and dance;
Boys: Praise him with strings and pipe!
Girls: Praise him with sounding cymbals;
Boys: Praise him with loud clashing cymbals!
All: Let everything that breathes praise the Lord!
All: Praise the Lord!

> Make copies of an antiphonal, or response/echo, song. Assign parts. Color-code each line. "Sing Hosannas" is given below as an example (see p. 143). Another good example is "All Creatures of Our God and King."

Blue: Hark to the story angels are telling
        Of the birth of Jesus
Red: Born in a manger mid cattle lowly
        Is the Babe most holy
Blue: Sing, all ye angels,
Red: Sing, all ye shepherds!
Both: Sing to the little Babe in the manger
Blue: Sing a soft hosanna,
Red: Sing a loud hosanna,
All: Jesus Christ is born today.

PROCEDURE

Use the following activities separately or in any combination:

• Make musical instruments.

Cymbals: Use 2 metal pot lids.

Tambourines or timbrels: Fill an aluminum pie plate with dried beans. Place another plate on top. Staple around the edges. Thread 16 gold bells through narrow Christmas gift ribbon. Space bells evenly. Spread a thin layer of glue around the edge of the plates. Glue the ribbon and bells onto the plates. Use a toothpick to hold the ribbon in place. Allow time to dry. For more decoration, glue or staple ball fringe over the ribbon, attaching it close under the bells.

Rhythm sticks: Sand and paint dowel sticks.

Harps: Stretch rubberbands over the tops of greeting card boxes or cake pans.

Drums: Remove the lids from empty coffee cans or oatmeal boxes. Stretch scraps of leather over the ends. Fasten leather securely around the edges with cord.

Sand blocks: Staple or tack sandpaper to wooden blocks.

• Sing the verses of a song. Ask the children to join in on the chorus.

• Ask the children to close their eyes and listen to a song. Then ask them to tell what they heard. Or, ask specific questions about the song.

• Display the words of a song on a window shade. Roll it up when not in use.

• Play a song that may be too difficult for children to sing, but that could create a mood, for example, "The God of Abraham Praise" (see p. 174).

- Plan a praise service using an "orchestra" of home-made instruments (see p. 143). Add autoharps, zithers (can be purchased at a toy store), triangles, rhythm bells, and other simple instruments.

- Display the sign. As the children arrive, play several taped songs that deal with the same subject.

- Show pictures illustrating a certain song. Sing the song repeatedly. Ask the children to arrange the pictures in order. Then, using pictures, only sing the song.

- Select songs that have been taken from biblical text. Read the verses from the Bible. Ask the children to decide on the meaning of the verses. Then sing the song.

- Display the song rebus. Allow children to draw or glue on pictures. Then, using the rebus, sing the song.

- Dramatize a song. Choose children to play-act certain phrases.

- Make a songbook. Add to it the words of songs that are not ordinarily found in hymnals.

- Lead children in singing a song based on a psalm. Ask, **What do you think happened to the writer of the psalm that inspired him to write this song?** Discuss answers. Sing the song again.

- Sing only the part of a song you need to teach a truth.

- Use secular music that isn't offensive or opposed to Bible teachings to set a mood. For example: Play Grofe's *Grand Canyon Suite*, particularly "Cloud-burst," when working on a study of nature, ecology, the world, or creation. When studying about Joseph, play selections from the musical *Joseph and the Amazing Technicolor Dreamcoat*.

- Ask the organist to play a song appropriate to the study. Ask the children to sing along. Let the organist demonstrate sounds the organ will produce.

- Add your own words to a familiar tune. For example, to "Here We Go Round the Mulberry Bush," add either "This is the way we bake our bread," "This is the way a donkey sounds," or "This is the way a carpenter works."

- Ask the children to pantomime how the music makes them feel.

- Help the children to write an original song. Use a familiar 4-line tune. Ask each child to write 4 new lines. Start singing the song. Ask each child to "jump in" and sing her own verse.

- Sing a song with the children. Ask them to draw something they sang about.

- Sing a familiar song several times until everyone joins in.

- Invent a 2-line song with a pretty melody. Ask the children to add 2 lines that fit the melody. Ask everyone to sing the lines together. Continue to add original lines. Sing the song together.

- Ask some children to go to the Searching Stop to find information on music used in synagogues and in different periods of Christian history.

- Before you sing a song, give background information about the writing of it.

- Ask the children to think of songs related to the present study. Sing at least 1 of the songs together.

- Invite an instrumental or vocal soloist to present music related to the present study.

- Ask the children to listen carefully to the words of a song. Ask them what words in the song remind them of a certain thing, for instance, God's promise or a dangerous place.

- With hymnals closed, ask the children to listen to a song melody. Ask, **How did you like the melody? Now let's look at the words and see if they fit what you just heard. Then let's sing it.**

- Sing 1-part songs with a melody in the voice range of both boys and girls.

- Sing a phrase of a song. Ask the children to sing it back to you.

- Instruct the children to look through a hymnal and write the names of at least 5 songs that relate to a certain topic, for example, prayer.

- Use body percussion with a song such as "Praise Him, Praise Him, All Ye Little Children." For example: Clap hands on count 1; snap fingers on count 2. Raise hands on count 1; pat hands on count 2. Put hands on lap on count 1; snap fingers on count 2. Slap hands on counts 1 and 2.

- Ask the children to put a plastic plumber's elbow to their ears and mouth and sing to themselves.

- Read aloud the words of a song before you sing it.

- Ask a child to play a drumbeat accompaniment to the singing.

- Assign parts for the reading of Psalm 150. Send the boys to an area of the room and girls to another area. Read responsively. Ask, ***Does this psalm make you think about the greatness of God? Can you name the musical instruments that are mentioned? How many of these are used in your service of worship?*** Show illustrations of some of the instruments named in this psalm. Share background information on how they were made and used (see p.143).

- Divide the children into 2 or more groups. Assign them to different areas of the room. Have 1 group echo every other line of an antiphonal song.

- Sing a song in rounds: A group sings a phrase. Another group joins in and sings the first phrase. Another group joins in with the first phrase. Each group repeats the song until the end, with the third group ending last. [Example: "Come, Let Us Gather," *Songs for Children* (Nashville: Broadman Press, 1964) 170.]

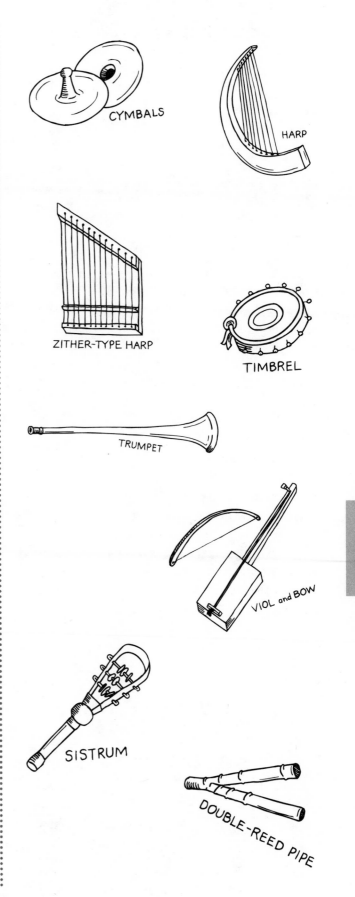

CYMBALS

HARP

ZITHER-TYPE HARP

TIMBREL

TRUMPET

VIOL and BOW

SISTRUM

DOUBLE-REED PIPE

PRAISING

Prayer Activities

RESOURCES
chalk
chalk/markerboard
felt tip pen
paper

PREPARATION
> Prepare the following charts:

Types of Prayers

- prayers of thanksgiving (Psalm 9:1-2)
- prayers on the behalf of others (Romans 1:9)
- prayers requesting a favor (Psalm 25:4)
- prayers expressing deep feelings (Psalm 27:7-9)
- prayers of praise (Psalm 8:1)
- prayers of repentance (Psalm 51)
- prayers of trust (Psalm 23:1)
- prayers for courage (Psalm 56:3)

Prayer Starters

- "God, I don't know what to do about . . . "
- "I'm afraid that . . . Can you help me?"
- "There's something I know I shouldn't do, but I want to do it anyway."
- "Today I saw an eclipse of the sun. Thank you, God, for showing me that. Thanks also for . . . "
- "It's about that girl I don't like . . . "
- "God, I'm sorry for . . . "
- "I love you, God . . . "

Ways to Pray

- Pray silently.
- Use conversational prayer.
- Pray a feeling prayer.
- Offer an eyes-open prayer.
- Pray a written prayer.
- Read a Bible passage prayer.

PROCEDURE
Use the following activities separately or in any combination:

- Ask, *Where are some places we can pray?* List responses on paper or chalk/markerboard. Include some of the following if the children don't name them: in your warm and cozy bed, on a grassy spot under a big tree, on the limb of a big tree, in a swing, in the park or on a playground, at the table where you eat, in a vehicle while you travel, anywhere.

- Ask the children to help you think of different types of prayer. Add responses to the prepared chart. Discuss the types listed. Read the Scriptures listed. Encourage the children to use different kinds of prayers. Say, *Some of the prayers listed on the chart were prayed by a man who often felt as you do. He was scared, lonely, afraid, sorry for something, thankful, and sometimes even angry.*

- Ask, *When you pray, do you sometimes have a difficult time getting started? Why don't you try these prayer starters?* Point to the chart. Choose one of the prayer starters. Start the prayer. Lead the children to pray together as a group.

- Say, *An echo prayer repeats a phrase several times. Turn in your Bibles to Psalm 136, which is an echo prayer. What is the echo phrase in this psalm? Let's read this psalm together as a prayer.*

Explain the following ways to pray, and then demonstrate them together:

Pray silently. Just think about something you would like to happen without voicing it to God aloud.

Use conversational prayer. Members of a group may enter into the group's conversation with God anytime they wish. They may express one idea or several ideas. They may thank God for something or pray for someone else. The leader closes it.

Pray a feeling prayer from your heart instead of a memorized prayer such as "Now I lay me down to sleep."

Offer an eyes-open prayer. Look at others while you pray for them.

Pray a written prayer. These are fine to use if they are sincere. You also may pray someone else's written prayer.

Read a Bible passage prayer, such as Psalm 61. Make it your own prayer as you read it. Then name things you want to thank God for.

PRAISING

Chapter 15
CARING: Participating in Ministry Activities

Rationale

There are many crises and much stress in the lives of children and their parents. Much of the stress seems to be related to separation: divorce, a new baby who takes a parent's time, the feeling of being left out when a parent remarries, hospitalization, the death of a pet, a move to another location, homelessness, the illness or death of a family member.

Often people are disturbed, unhappy, isolated, lonely, disadvantaged, struggling, and stressed out. Unfortunately, children must live in the midst of all of this. They need help, but they're aware that others need help, too. They can be taught to care for and share with others. Caring concern can help children develop a healthy self-esteem. With proper guidance, they can become committed to a life of serving. This chapter includes suggested ministry activities children can do.

Sample Ministry Lessons

SHARING WITH OUR FAMILIES

RESOURCES
broom
chairs
chalk
chalk/markerboard
dish drainer
felt tip pens
garbage can
Handiwipes
hassock
ironing board
paper
paper plates
pencils
pillows
rug
stool

PREPARATION
> Make copies of "My Family" (see p. 155).

PROCEDURE
Ask the children to help move items into the area to create a home scene. Say, ***There are very few places where we are asked to share more than we do in our homes with our own families. Suggest some things we need to share there.*** The children may suggest: responsibility, the love of parents and siblings, space, sadness, joy, "things" that belong to everyone (television, games, furniture, food). List responses on paper or chalk/markerboard. Ask, ***Does it sometimes become a problem to share? Does it create conflict when people must live closely together? During biblical times the family included practically everyone—aunts, uncles, grandparents, servants, animals, etc.***

Distribute "My Family" worksheets to the children. Ask them to complete the statements. Allow them time to share their answers with the group if they wish. Remind them that there may be answers they don't want to share.

Guide children in role-playing a family conflict situation. Ask different children to assume the following roles: father, mother, sister, 2 brothers. Present a problem, for instance, the children don't want to participate in a family outing. All family members will be allowed to say whatever they wish to the others about the problem. Encourage all children to watch the facial expressions, words, and body movements of the characters. Allow the action to go on for a few minutes. Then stop the action. Ask the rest of the group to react to what they've seen and heard. Ask the group to share better solutions to the problem.

Assign: *Watch a family show on TV. Record on paper the conflict, how the family resolved the conflict, and the good and bad things you saw in the show. Plan to share your report in the next class session.* (You may wish to choose a particular show and also request cooperation from parents.)

Ask the children to mention things in families that cause stress. They may suggest: living with single parents, living in a blended family, death, drugs, violence, fear, financial problems, divorce, favoritism, rules that are too strict, the pressure to succeed at school or in sports, the addiction of a parent, and jealousy. Ask the children what they do when these stressors are present. (Encourage them to keep their answers private if they wish.) They may suggest:

- I scream and yell, "You aren't fair."
- I just leave the room and go off by myself. Then I don't talk to anyone for a long time.
- I get very angry, but then I try to see their side.
- I say, "You never let me do what I want to do. You just don't love me."

- I get very disappointed, but I tell myself that things will be different next time.
- I think to myself, "I'm not surprised. I expect these bad things to happen to me. They've happened before."
- I just pretend it isn't happening. I shut it out.

Ask, *Of all these actions, what is probably the worst you can do? Is it important to express your feelings?*

Ask the children to stand. Present the following situations. Say, *Take 1 step forward when you think you are the answer to the question. Be honest.*

- Who refused to clean the bathroom?
- Who watched TV while Mom was bringing in the groceries?
- Who broke a dish and quickly hid it in the garbage can?
- Who got busy when it was time to take out the garbage?
- Who cleaned your room only halfway?
- Who raked the leaves as quickly as possible so you could go on to something else?
- Who growled when you had to take care of your younger brother or sister?
- Who yelled at your brother or sister when he or she broke something of yours?

Ask, *Does conflict often result because of responsibilities in the family that aren't being taken care of? Then, would you say that sometimes the fault is yours and you might be the cause of the conflict? Your parents have good reason for giving you chores. It allows them some free time for fun and also teaches you how to do those chores well in the future.*

Place a dish drainer on the floor. Insert a paper plate in each section. Ask several children to choose a paper plate and write on it how they can better help at home. Read their answers aloud. Then place the plates in the dish drainer. Pass around Handiwipes and felt tip pens to the other children in the room. Ask them to write on the Handiwipes what they can do to be better helpers at home. Read their answers aloud.

Ask the children to write a rap about families. A rap is a poem with sets of 2 rhyming lines. It is chanted in rhythm like this:

Now listen to me, friends, about a terrible plight.
But quick-thinking Isaac, he avoided a fight.

WE ARE ALL MINISTERS

RESOURCES
Bible translations (NRSV, TEV, KJV)

PREPARATION
> Invite as a special guest someone whom you consider to be a servant/minister.

PROCEDURE
Ask the children to name a few Bible characters who helped others. Ask, *What does the word "minister" mean? Jesus gave a good definition in Matthew 20:27-28.* Ask 3 children to read these verses from each of the following Bible translations: New Revised Standard Version (NRSV), Today's English Version (TEV), King James Version (KJV). Ask, *Who was the Son of Man? In what ways did he minister to others? Can you think of another word for minister? Now that you know the definition, do you think all of us can be ministers?*

Share these character sketches:

Linley Forbis is a senior adult. He serves his church as a carpenter/woodworker. He has made blocks and toys for the nursery and preschool groups, doorstops to hold the doors open, replicas of Noah's ark and the animals for display in the church library, and rods for hanging costumes. He asks for no money; he does his work because he loves God. Would you call him a modern-day "Joseph of Nazareth?" Would you call him a minister?

Louise Duke is a church member who saw the need in her city for a soup kitchen where church members could cook for and feed the hungry, the poor, and street persons. Would you call her a minister?

Tell the children about the ways the guest helps others. Then ask the guest questions such as these: *Would you call yourself a minister? Why is your job/responsibility/contribution important to you? Do you get any rewards from helping others?* Remember, the guest may be very humble in his/her responses; true servants are.

Say, *We can all be servants. Ever since the world began, people have needed help from each other.*

MINISTERS IN THE EARLY CHURCH

RESOURCES
Bibles
felt tip pens
paper

PREPARATION
> Print these Scripture references on strips of paper: Acts 3:1-8, Acts 4:32-35, Acts 5:12, Acts 9:32-34, Acts 11:27-30. Hide the paper strips somewhere in the room.

PROCEDURE
Ask the children to find the Scripture references. When they have found all 5 references, ask them to read these in their Bibles and tell how those members of the early church served and helped others. Answers follow:

- Acts 3:1-8 (Peter and John healed a lame man.)
- Acts 4:32-35 (The Christians sold their belongings and shared the money with each other.)
- Acts 5:12 (The apostles performed miracles and wonders for the people.)
- Acts 9:32-34 (Peter healed Aeneas.)
- Acts 11:27-30 (The Christians of Antioch sent money to the believers in Judea to help them.)

Say, *There were probably no orphanages, so children without parents had to be cared for. Widows could not earn a living, so they also had to be cared for. New Testament churches had unexpected suffering and trouble just as churches do today. People needed help. How can you and I do some of the things the people in these verses did? Sometimes all we can do is pray. Are we servants if all we do is pray?*

Share these character sketches:

Orestes Hernandez is a retired Cuban Baptist pastor. For many years, while mentally alert, he awakened at 3 A.M. in the morning and prayed until 7 A.M. He kept a thick notebook with names of people from all over the world for whom he felt the need to pray. Would you call him a minister?

A 4th grader named Anne sat in a prayer meeting with her parents. She heard about a woman whose husband had just died. She took a card and wrote a simple message. It said: "I am so sorry that you are so sad. Love, Anne." The church mailed her card. Could you write a simple message that would help someone?

Ask the children to name persons who need prayer. Spend a few moments praying for them.

Class Activities

RESOURCES
paper
pencils
table paper
tape

PREPARATION
> Enlarge "Ways I Can Minister" (see p. 156) to poster size.

> Hang table paper (doubled) on the wall.

> Make copies of "Helping in Our Church Family" (see p. 157).

PROCEDURE
Use the following activities separately or in any combination:

- Display the poster of "Ways I Can Minister." Ask the children to suggest ways they can minister in each situation. List responses in the blanks.

- Assign a friend/buddy for each new child who comes to your group. Ask the friend to take him around, sit with him, introduce him to others, and so on.

- Ask the children to write an "Add-a-Sentence Letter" to someone who needs encouragement. Deliver the letter.

- Ask the children to draw on table paper several streets in their town or around the church. On each street, draw houses, stores, and other buildings. Write the names of people who need help, for example, the sick man next door, the man who owned the bakery shop that closed for lack of business, Mrs. _____ whose husband just died, the _____ family whose house burned. Then discuss with the children how they as individuals and/or a group can help these persons.

- Ask the children to complete the worksheet "Helping in Our Church Family."

Out-of-Class Group Activities

RESOURCES
bags or boxes
duplicate picture
felt tip pens
items for travel bags
items for a sick child's box
table paper
VCR
videotape

PREPARATION

> Set up videotaping equipment.

> Plan a scavenger hunt to collect food staples.
> Collect items for children's travel bags.

> Collect items for a box to give to a sick child.

> Ask a group of parents, leaders, and children to sleep overnight in a park. Ask them to bring a cardboard box to sleep on or inside and very few necessities.

> Plan a scavenger hunt for prospects. Give assignments such as this: Bring a boy or girl who lives at _____, has brown hair and blue eyes, and goes to _____ School.

> Obtain permission from a hospital and the personnel there for your group to visit the children's ward.

> Obtain the names of children whose parents are in prison.

> Find a picture duplicate.

PROCEDURE

Use the following activities separately or in any combination:

• Videotape a Christmas program. Take it to a sick child.

• Make a videotape of your group's activities. Take it to a prospect.

• Go on a scavenger hunt to collect food items. Take these to a family in need.

• Assemble travel bags for children going on vacation. Include items such as: Bible verses, games and stories from outdated curriculum, homemade or inexpensive games, a postcard to mail back to the group, sticks of sugarless gum, a small notebook and pencil to record events of the trip.

• Make a goody box to send to a sick child. Include such items as simple games, sugarless gum, crossword puzzles, tissues, candy, a page of jokes, a small mirror, comb, cologne, and other items.

• After sleeping in the park, ask, *How did it feel to be homeless? How did it feel to have no place to cook, or brush your teeth? How would it feel to look forward to this situation day after day?* Talk about ways you can help the homeless.

• Cover tables with paper in preparation for a church meal. Decorate the table coverings with felt tip pens and a caring message.

• Plan a party. The ticket to get in is to bring a prospect.

• Go on a scavenger hunt for prospects. Then enjoy a social time.

• Visit a prospect. Then go out together for ice cream or another treat.

• Read books to the patients in the children's ward of a hospital.

• Adopt as friends the families of persons in prison. Minister to them at various times throughout the year.

• Cut a picture into puzzle parts. Send a piece of the puzzle, along with the following note, to several prospects you would like to see join your group. Put the puzzles together when the prospects arrive.

Dear _____:
Please be a part of the picture when our group gets together again on (date) at (time and place). If you come, our picture will be complete. If not, you'll be missed, and our puzzle will not be complete. Please bring your piece with you.

CARING

Out-of-Class Individual Activities

RESOURCES
items to take to various persons
paper
pencils
postcards
stamps

PREPARATION
> Collect/prepare items to take to various persons.

> Make a list of activities/assignments.

PROCEDURE
Encourage the children to do the following activities on their own:

- Visit elderly persons. Take treats, magazines, and newspapers to them.

- Remember your parents by making and taking them breakfast in bed on holidays and birthdays.

- Write good memories from your childhood. Give them to your parents.

- Offer to feed pets, water flowers, or check on grandparents while a family goes on vacation.

- Take food to a family who needs it and/or take a recipe and the ingredients to make it.

- Invite children who live in an apartment building to play in your yard.

- Read a story to, or write a letter for, an elderly person whose eyesight is failing.

- Help a single mom give a birthday party for her child.

- Help international students with their homework.

- Write a note of congratulations to someone for a particular achievement.

- Write postcards to absentees.

- Write letters to the custodians and kitchen staff in the building where you meet. Thank them for their hard work.

- If your church has a food ministry, assist adults in filling grocery bags, chopping fruits and vegetables, setting up tables, and cleaning up. Print Bible verses on the bags and/or include literature.

- Take homemade treats and cards to shut-ins.

- Clean out your closets. Collect clothes, shoes, toys, games, and books you no longer use. Give these to a family in need.

- Collect used baby clothing and equipment to take to a shelter or to a needy family with a new baby.

- Call a friend when her pet dies.

- Talk with and encourage a friend who is hurting inside. Remember, what you discuss is a secret between the two of you.

My Family

Complete the following statements:

A sister should:

My father never:

My mother says:

I hate it when:

My family:

I love the times when we:

I'm afraid:

A brother should never:

Ways I Can Minister

Complete the following statements.

When I see new people at church who can't find their age group, I can:

When my leader is going into a building and trying to carry too much, I can:

When I'm told that my class is being divided and I will have a new leader, I can:

When someone drops food at a meal that could cause someone else to slip and fall, I can:

When my leader gives me more work to do than he gives to anyone else, I can:

When an elderly person is going into the building and must climb many steps, I can:

When it's time to leave the class and the leader says, "It's time to put away supplies," I can:

When I see a handicapped person, I can:

When I pass by a lonely elderly person, I can:

When I see a child at school or church or on the playground who seems to have no friends, I can:

When I see someone on crutches or in a wheelchair, I can:

When the parents of someone at school or church are going through a divorce, I can:

When a new child moves into my neighborhood, I can:

When my friend is really disappointed or hurting, I can:

When a family is being hurt by rumors and gossip, I can:

Helping in Our Church Family

Here is a list of things that could happen in your church family. What could you do to help? Write your answers in the blanks.

Someone has an accident

_____

A wedding is held

_____

A family is homeless

_____

A new baby is born

_____

Someone is ill

_____

Someone dies

_____

Someone makes a bad mistake and goes to jail or prison

_____

Someone loses a job and can't find another one

_____

Someone is hurting inside for whatever reason

_____

Grandparents have grandchildren who live far away, and they miss them

_____

Chapter 16
PLAYING: Engaging in Recreation That Teaches

Rationale

Fun times together out of class offer opportunities for learning and/or applying biblical principles and for bonding between the children themselves and with their leaders. What better and more fun way to get to know each other than through recreation? Recreation brings together children from different schools, neighborhoods, backgrounds, and family situations. Playing can break down barriers and provide acceptance for all. This chapter gives examples of trips, games, and other organized events that can help children learn as they play.

Desert Wanderings Camping Trip

RESOURCES
*see "Items to Take" (p. 160)
biscuits (canned or prepared mix)
blindfolds
candy (40 pieces)
cardboard
cassette player
cassette tapes
charcoal
clothespins
construction paper
cooking utensils
felt tip pens
honey
horn
ingredients for meals and snacks (see recipes)
knives
lighter fluid
map
matches
measuring spoons
milk
nametags
paper
paper products
pencils
pins
rice cakes
sandals
scissors
shoe polish
shophar or trumpet
snacks
sticks
string or tape
tents
whistle

Holy Hobo Popcorn (recipe serves 1)

aluminum foil (heavy duty)
cooking oil
popcorn kernels

In the center of a square of heavy foil, place 1 tsp. oil and 1 TBS. popcorn kernels. Bring foil corners together. Make a pouch. Pinch edges together. Allow room for expansion. With string, tie the pouch to a long stick. Place the pouch directly on hot coals. Shake constantly until popcorn is popped.

Serpent on a Rod[1]

biscuit dough
flour
shaved sticks
tin cans

Prepare a biscuit recipe or use canned biscuits or a prepared mix. Roll dough out on floured paper with a tin can. Cut rolled dough into narrow 1/2" strips. Wrap dough on a shaved stick, overlapping the ends and pinching them to secure the dough to the stick. (Don't let the dough spirals touch each other; this will slow down the cooking time.) Bake over coals or charcoal. Variation: For cinnamon twists, add 2 TBS. of brown sugar. When baked, brush with melted margarine, and roll in cinnamon and sugar mix (4 parts sugar to 1 part cinnamon).

Traveler's Sandwich

cheese
French bread
lettuce
luncheon meats
mayonnaise
mustard
pickles
tomatoes

Place sandwich items on French bread. Slice into servings. Serve with chips, cookies, and juice.

Wilderness Burgers (recipe serves 4)

1 lb. ground beef
1/2 c. chopped onions
1 can chicken gumbo soup
1/2 c. water
2 tsp. chili sauce
1 tsp. prepared mustard
salt
hamburger buns

Brown meal and onions in skillet. Drain. Add soup and water. Add chili sauce, prepared mustard, and salt to taste. Cook 30-40 minutes on low or medium. Serve on buns. Examples of these follow.

PREPARATION

> Select a site for the campout, one with a swimming pool.

> Obtain supplies needed for the trip.

> Arrange for transportation.

> Print and distribute to parents and children copies of a list of items to take, the camp schedule, and a medical/permission form.

Items to Take

$___ for food
bandanna
Bible
camp schedule
clothing (1 extra outfit)
fruit (1 piece)
hiking shoes
insect repellent
jacket
medical/permission form
personal hygiene items
sleeping bag
swimsuit and towel

PLAYING

Camp Schedule

Friday:
4:00   Meet at _____. Enjoy a snack.
4:30   Depart
5:30   Unpack. Heat Wilderness Burgers.
         Set up tents.
6:30   Supper
7:00   Cleanup
7:30   Hike (Carry the Ark of the Covenant with you [see Numbers 10:33]. Transporters go first. Everyone else follows.)
8:30   Bible study
9:15   Bonfire, Singing, Prayertime, Holy Hobo Popcorn
10:00   PHT* *personal hygiene time*
10:30   Lights Out

Saturday:
8:00   Breakfast
8:30   Cleanup and PHT*
9:00   Bible Study
10:00   Scavenger Hunt
10:30   Games, Hiking, General Fun
12:30   Lunch and Cleanup
1:00   Moving On . . . Cleaning Out
2:00   Crossing the Red Sea
3:30   Leave for home
4:30   Arrive at _____.

Medical/Permission Form

(child's name) _____ has my permission to attend (event) _____ on (date) _____.
I do not hold (name of church or group) _____ or the leaders responsible for accidents. I authorize accompanying adults to make emergency medical decisions concerning my child.

    (parent's signature) _____
    (phone number) _____
    (date) _____

> Practice setting up tents.

> Ask some children to make a cardboard replica of the Ark of the Covenant as described in Exodus 25:10-22.

> Make specific work assignments: cooking, cleaning up, finding fuel for a fire, setting up tents, cooking one's own food, and so on.

> Print and make copies of the following list of items children are to find in a scavenger hunt.

- bark
- dried leaf
- green moss
- litter
- rock 3" wide
- round rock
- something in nature you haven't seen before
- stick (Y-shaped)
- white rock
- wildflower

> Make small cardboard cutouts of grapes, pomegranates, and figs.

> Make cardboard replicas of a rod and a staff.

> Shave the bark off the end of a stick for each child.

> Prepare Wilderness Burgers.

PROCEDURE

Meet at the place of departure. Serve a snack. Review the camp schedule. Depart.

Set up the campsite. Distribute construction paper, felt tip pens, scissors, and clothespins. Each tent group is to post an insignia that identifies itself as housing for 1 of the following tribes: Judah, Isaachar, Zebulun, Reuben, Simeon, Gad, Levi, Joseph, Benjamin, Dan, Asher, Naphtali.

PLAYING

Reheat Wilderness Burgers. Serve with lemonade or pop and the fruit the children brought. Clean up. Take a hike.

Study together Deuteronomy 8:15 and Numbers 11:4-7. Show the children a large map of the journey of the Israelites. Say, *This was a difficult trip in a terrible wilderness. The only food was manna day after day, but later God sent them quails to eat.* See Numbers 11:31. *There was very little water.* See Exodus 15:22. *How hard would it be to find water in the Sinai desert? What did Moses do about it?* See Exodus 15:22-25. *There were poisonous snakes in the desert.* See Numbers 21:6. *The weather was hot and dry. There was no place to take a bath. Moses had to keep up with about 600,000 men, in addition to the women, children, and animals. What other problems would the Israelites have had on this trip?*

Distribute pencils and paper. Ask the group to review the Ten Commandments in Exodus 20 and then to state them positively instead of negatively. Ask why God felt it was so important to give these rules. Then make up a set of positive rules for this camping trip.

Make a campfire. Sing, pray, and make Holy Hobo Popcorn. Then prepare for bedtime.

Blow a shophar (ram's horn) for a wake-up call. For breakfast serve only rice cakes and a little water. (Keep the menu a secret until breakfast.) When the children complain, remind them that the Israelites ate manna for 40 years. As you eat, talk about the manna and what it tasted and looked like. (See Exodus 16:4, 13, 15, 31). Ask, *How would you have liked to eat this for 40 years? Now do you understand why the people complained to Moses?* (Do promise the children a good lunch today!) Clean up.

Study Deuteronomy 8:7-10. Ask, *What would the land of Caanan be like when the people got there? What was God's purpose in this trip?*

Explain to the children that they are going on a scavenger hunt in "the wilderness." Distribute copies of the list of items they are to find.

Reassemble the group. Ask, *How many of the items you found on the scavenger hunt would you find in the Sinai desert? Was it pretty barren?*

Play games related to the Bible studies.

- *Promised Land Walk*—Draw a line on the ground, or use string or tape. Ask the children to stand behind the line. Station yourself at the front of the line 50 yards ahead. Turn your back to the group. Count *1-2-3-4-5-6-7-8-9-10-Caanan*. Then turn around quickly. If you see anyone moving, that person must get out of the game. The first person to reach you can enter the land of Caanan and receive a reward of milk and honey.

- *40 Years to Get There*—Draw a line on the ground. Divide the group into 2 teams. Position each team behind the line in single file. Give these instructions: *When I say "go," the 1st player will use any form of locomotion—walk, run, skip, hop, roll, crawl, somersault, walk backward or sideways—to move forward. The 2nd player will use a different movement. Play will continue in this way. The first team to have all of its players on the opposite side will win 40 pieces of candy.*

- *Who Is the Leader of This Trip?*—Ask a child to walk away and hide his eyes. While he is gone, choose someone to be Moses. Moses starts clapping or some other motion. The other players follow him, changing motions when Moses does. The person sent out tries to discover who Moses is. When he does, the leader is sent out, and the "guesser" becomes Moses. (The trick for the other players is not to look at Moses directly.)

- *Sandal Circle*—Ask the children to stand in a close circle. Appoint someone to be "It." The person who is "It" stands in the center of the circle. The children pass around a sandal in the back of the circle in either direction. "It" tries to locate the sandal. If she succeeds, the one in possession of the sandal takes her place.

- *Let My People Go*—Ask each child to make and wear a tag bearing only their last name. Go to each child in turn and say, **We're going to the "promised land." What will you take with you?** Only those children who answer correctly may go. Take them over to the side. (To go, players must take something with them that begins with the first letter of their last name.) "Sentence" those who don't catch on to polish sandals.

- *Stumbling Across Egypt*—Talk about how the Israelites complained in the desert and wanted to return to Egypt. Then choose 2 teams. Instruct the members of each team to choose partners, stand back to back, and link arms. At the signal to go, a player runs forward while his teammate runs backward until they reach the goal line. As soon as both teammates touch the goal line, they start back, reversing positions. Now the player who ran backward must run forward. The first team to have all players return wins.

- *Spies to the Promised Land*—Hide small cardboard cutouts of grapes, pomegranates, and figs. Tell a story based on Numbers 13. Ask the children to form a circle. Play music. Instruct them to march around in the circle until the music stops playing. At that point, they leave the circle and hunt the cardboard objects. When the music begins again, they must stop hunting, get back in the circle, and march until the music stops again. Play until all the objects are found.

- *Rod and Staff*—Position children in a circle. Show cardboard replicas of a rod and a staff. Appoint a child to be Moses. Ask him to stand at the head of the circle and pass an object to the person on his right and say, "This is a rod." The person receiving it says, "A what?" Moses repeats, "A rod." That player must pass it on to the next player, carrying on the same conversation. Each time, the question is passed all the way back to Moses, who answers,

"A rod." Meanwhile, Moses passes another object to his left and says, "This is a staff." The game becomes confusing when the 2 objects meet.

- *Para Iveret (Blind Cow)*—Blindfold all players except the "instructor." Ask the players to stand in a row in front of the "instructor" who calls out drills and marching instructions, which they must follow immediately. At any time she chooses, the "instructor" may blow a whistle, and the players must stop where they are. If played in several groups, the group having the best formation at the sound of the whistle wins the game. If the group is so small that only one group is used, the players farthest out of line can be eliminated each time the game is played.

Have each child make a Traveler's Sandwich and a Serpent on a Rod. Serve with chips and juice. Enjoy a time of swimming. Head home.

*PHT (personal hygiene time)

Summer Olympics

RESOURCES
bay leaves
Bibles (several translations)
bowls
food items (10)
felt tip pens
Frisbees
hats
horseshoes
ingredients for ice cream sundaes
(ice cream, toppings, whipped topping, cherries, nuts, etc.)
lunch items
paper
postage stamps
prizes
reference books
ropes
sticks (8)
table
table paper
tape
tape measure

PLAYING

PREPARATION

> Print and mail invitations to the children (see p. 169).

> Ask some children to do research in the Searching Stop on the Greek Olympic Games and then to help plan the event. You may wish to do this in connection with a study of the apostle Paul.

> Ask the children and leaders to bring sandwiches, drinks, chips, cookies, and their Bibles.

> Cut a piece of table paper 9'x30". Print this Scripture verse on the banner: "Athletes exercise self-control in all things" (1 Corinthians 9:25). Display it on the wall or, if outside, hang it between 2 trees.

> Print each of the following Scriptures on a separate piece of table paper.

- "In the case of an athlete, no one is crowned without competing according to the rules." (2 Timothy 2:5)
- "In a race, the runners all compete, but only one receives the prize." (1 Corinthians 9:24)
- "I have finished the race, I have kept the faith." (2 Timothy 4:7)
- "Let us run with perseverance the race that is set before us." (Hebrews 12:1)

> Hang a scripture banner over the gathering place of each group.

PROCEDURE

Appoint judges to keep an ongoing tally of every team's points. Divide the children into 4 teams. Have boys and girls on each team. Appoint a leader to be in charge of each team. Tell the leaders they will go to the center area for instructions for each event and then return to their groups to explain the event.

Ask the researchers to share their report about the Olympics. Add the following information if needed[2]:

A big part of every Greek boy's education was wrestling, discus and javelin throwing, running, and jumping sprints and relays. The Greeks had an admiration for well-developed bodies. They were the champions in athletics. The apostle Paul may have attended the Greek games celebrated every 3 years outside the city of Corinth, since he made many references in his Bible books to athletic contests. He made it clear that the Christian life is a race also.

Greek athletes trained for 10 months before the games. They gathered in a stadium for the events. The contests were wrestling, boxing, pitching quoits (similar to horseshoes), throwing the spear, and foot racing. The latter was the most important. Runners wore plumed helmets and ran with shields on their left arms.

The Romans were also good athletes. They raced with chariots in a large arena called a "circus." The largest of these arenas seated 150,000 people. People placed bets on their favorite charioteers. The Jews participated in athletic events as well. King Herod the Great sponsored chariot races and wrestling matches. He built a gymnasium at Caesarea.

Ask teams to participate in the following events:

- *The Best Trained*—Call the athletes to the center. Measure the waistlines of the members on each team. Add the inches to see which team has the smallest number, thereby being in the best physical condition. (Yes, they're allowed to "suck in.")

- *Gobble Relay*—Divide the children into 2 groups. Line them up in single file. Place a table at the end of each line. Place on each table the same number of articles of food as the number of players in the line. For instance, if there are 10 players in each line, each table might contain (1) a piece of cheese, (2) a piece of bread, (3) a spoonful of honey, (4) a small piece of melon, (5) a bite of tomato,

(6) a small cup of water, (7) a small piece of cucumber, (8) grapes cut in half, (9) a small box of raisins, and (10) a small sandwich bag of marshmallows. Give these instructions: *At the signal, the first player in each line runs to the table, takes her choice of foods, eats a food item completely at the table, and returns to touch off the second player. The winning team is the first to clear its table of food.*

- Ice Cream Olympics—Choose 2 teams. Place bowls and ingredients for ice cream sundaes at each end of a long table. Give these instructions: *At the "go" signal, send a team member to add 1 ingredient to the sundae. Continue to send players to add 1 ingredient until the sundae is complete.* The child who adds the last ingredient gets to eat the sundae (but keep this a secret until the end of the game).

- Extemporaneous Speech—Ask a leader to come up and speak for 3 minutes on the subject "How to Train for an Olympic Pillow Fight."

- Knock on Wood—Give these instructions: *Number off by 2s. Form 2 lines. The 1st person in each line must cross her fingers, turn around 3 times, run to the end of the room, and knock 3 times on wood such as a door, window, baseboard, or, if outside, a tree. This player then runs back to the line and touches the 2nd person, who does the same thing. The first line to finish wins.*

- The Hunt—Ask the event leader to sit at a table. Line up the 4 teams behind a boundary line opposite the event leader. Ask each group to elect a runner. Give these instructions: *The leader will call for each team to supply a certain thing* (examples: a shoestring, a live blond, a sock, a shirt, a shoe, a comb, a hairclasp, someone wearing blue, someone wearing brown, a leader in the room, a brunette). *The team will supply the "thing" and give it to the runner, who will take it to the leader. The runner who reaches the event leader first with the requested "thing" wins a point for her group. The group with the most points at the end of the "hunt" wins.*

- Discus Throwing—Say, *Discus throwing was one of the most popular events in the Greek games. The thrower stood in a circle measuring 8"x2½". He couldn't step outside the circle. He swung within the circle with his arm outstretched. He released the discus at the end of the 2nd turn. He fouled if he touched the ground outside the circle with any part of his body or if he stepped on the circle. The distance was measured from the edge of the circle to the point where the discus struck the ground. Good form was a matter of practice rather than strength.* Measure off a circle with tape. Have the teams compete by throwing Frisbees.

- Jumping Jacks—Set up 2 sets of 4 rows of thin sticks. Divide the children into 2 equal groups. Line them up in single file. Give these instructions: *In turn, hop on 1 foot over each of the sticks to the end of the row. Then, while still hopping, start back. At the same time, stoop and pick up each stick after hopping over it. If you drop it, or if both feet touch the floor, you are disqualified. Replace the sticks each time. The winner is the 1st group to have all children return.*

- Foot Race—Remind the children that the foot race was the most important event of all the competition in the Greek games. Enlist 2 judges who have a watch with a second hand. Divide the children into 2 teams. Station them behind a boundary line. Give these instructions: *At the "go" signal, race to the finish line. The next person in line cannot start until the person in front crosses the line and her race time is tallied. The team with the smallest score wins.*

- Without Hands—Divide the children into 2 groups of 4 or 5 each. Ask the members of each group to stand in a row and hold a rope in front of them with both hands. A little distance away from each group, place on the floor the same number of hats as children. Give these instructions: *When the signal is given, each group, still holding the rope, will run toward its pile of hats. Each player on the team will try to get a hat on her head with-*

PLAYING

out the help of her hands. If any player uses her hands or drops the rope, the whole team will be disqualified. You may help each other by using your head, teeth, and feet. The group that returns to its place 1st, wearing hats, is the winner.

- *Quoits*—Play a game of horseshoes.

Call the children to bring their Bibles to the center area. Talk about prizes. Total the score of all the events to see which group is the winner. Award prizes. Ask the winning team to read aloud together the Scripture verses posted. Say, **In the Greek games, at the end of the foot race, the judge removed the winner's helmet from his head and crowned him with the wreath of pine leaves.**[3] **Winners also were crowned with laurel (myrtle) wreaths (1 Corinthians 9:25). In the time of the Greeks and Romans, the bay tree was known as the laurel, and its leaves were awarded to victors in the Olympic games and to heroes returning from war.**[4] Show some bay leaves. Let the children smell them. It was from this leaf that the wreaths were made. Give bay leaves to some of the winners of today's events.

Assign the following Scripture verses to be read in several translations:

- 2 Timothy 4:7, 8—Ask, **What do you think Paul meant by these verses? Was he comparing his life to a race?**
- Hebrews 12:1—Ask, **What is perseverance? What was Paul saying we should do?**
- Philippians 3:13b-14—Explain that this verse reflects an athletic event, a fast race. Ask, **Are you surprised that Paul used athletic events to describe the Christian life? Was he talking about a hard-fought race? What race? Who is our greatest rival in the game? What is our prize?**

Eat lunch.

Trip to the Zoo

RESOURCES
paper
pencils

PREPARATION

> Arrange a trip to the zoo.

> Review information on animals in biblical times.

> Make copies of "Animals of the Bible" (see p. 170). Answers are given for leaders.

(1) 9 gallons
(2) Their feet are tough and designed for the desert.
(3) wool for clothing, skin for coats, horns for shophars
(4) tabernacle and waterbags
(5) rich and poor
(6) to pull chariots, battles in wartime
(7) no
(8) false
(9) no
(10) yes
(11) cat
(12) Isaac
(13) food
(14) for special celebrations

PROCEDURE

Talk about the upcoming trip to the zoo. Give this background information:

Many kinds of animals are referred to in the Bible. Some of them were considered "beasts of burden." In other words, they carried heavy loads and transported people. Among these were camels and donkeys. Horses and elephants were used for similar purposes. Other animals were raised to provide food, milk, and material for making things and also to offer as sacrifices to God. Some of these were sheep, goats, cattle, deer, and various birds. Other animals mentioned in the Bible include lions, foxes, bears, leopards, vultures, ravens or crows, and eagles.

Arabian camels were used during biblical times. These have 1 hump on their backs. The hump is used for carrying heavy loads. Camels can drink as much as 9 gallons of water at a single drink and store it for several days. They can also store food in their humps. In biblical times, they drank from a leather trough. They ate the short straw they found on the threshing floors and also shrubs. Camels have the perfect feet for desert travel, with 2 long toes that sit on hard elastic cushions. Their feet are tough and do not sink or burn in the hot desert sand. They make very little noise as they walk.[5]

Camels are so tall, they must kneel for someone to get on their backs. Warts on their legs and chests serve as cushions when they kneel. First they drop on their knees, then on the joints of their hind legs, then on their chests, and finally on their bent hind legs. When they get up, this procedure is reversed. Camel riders take a camel stick, a leather bag with food, a leather apron, a camel saddle, and large saddlebags to carry equipment. Often people put ornaments or bells on their camels.

Camel caravans were used often in biblical times. A donkey always headed the procession. Following the donkey was a string of camels, each one tied to the one in front of it. Caravans always brought news. Since there were no newspapers, radios, or TVs, people looked forward to their coming. Jews did not eat camel meat, but they may have drunk the milk. Camel hair was woven into thread and often made into clothing, tents, and carpets. You may remember that John the Baptist wore clothing made of camel's hair.

Donkeys were used to carry supplies and also all kinds of people, including rich and poor. Jesus rode on a donkey during his triumphal

entry into Jerusalem. When women rode on donkeys, men sometimes acted as drivers. The milk of donkeys was also used. Donkeys can go for long periods without water, work hard in hot weather, and don't need much food. They are known for their stubbornness.

Horses were owned by the wealthy people and the government. They were used to pull chariots. When the Israelites left Egypt, the Bible tells us they were pursued by "all the horses and chariots of Pharaoh." King David and King Solomon used horses for fighting battles.

Elephants lived in biblical times, but apparently not in the land of Israel. They were valued for their ivory, which was brought in from Asian elephants.[6]

Sheep are spoken of often in the Bible. They were used for sacrifices more than any other animal. They were also used for their wool. People made coats from the woolen material and sometimes from the skin. The horns were also valuable. The left horn of a fat-tailed sheep was used to make a ram's horn, or shophar. Sheep ate green grass, so a shepherd was always watching for new pasture land. If sheep strayed away from the flock, they lost all sense of direction and often got lost or fell over cliffs. A shepherd then took his staff, which was usually crooked on the end and about 5' or 6' long, put it around the sheep, and lifted them out.

Most people in biblical times had goats. Goats were black, brown, or white. They were stubborn and difficult to control. Goats were used for their milk, meat, and skin and also as sacrifices. The hair and skin of goats were used to make the tabernacle. The skins were used for making leather, which in turn was used for making water bags and tents. Goat skin was especially good for making tents because when it rained, the skin shrunk, making the tent waterproof.[7]

Cattle were used as sacrifices and sometimes for meat. A "fatted calf"—usually not referred to as cattle—was a young cow that was fattened for the purpose of being eaten during a special celebration. See Luke 15:23.

The Israelites hunted different kinds of deer. It was venison, or deer meat, that Isaac asked Esau to bring him. Deer also are mentioned several times in the Psalms.

Doves and pigeons were also popular among the Israelites as food sources and sacrifices. God gave quail to the Israelites to eat, along with manna, during their desert wanderings to Caanan. See Exodus 16:13. *Wall paintings in Egyptian tombs show that the people caught these birds in nets for food.*

References in the Bible to some animals are not very complimentary. Lions, foxes, bears, and leopards were threats to small animals and to humans. People who followed God were sometimes put into a den of lions or had to fight them in an arena. Foxes were considered a nuisance. Because they, like the leopards of the cat family, could run at rapid speeds, they stole food such as fruit and eggs. Vultures and ravens are not spoken well of in the Bible because they search for dead animals, as opposed to eagles, which represent power and strength.

Take a trip to the zoo. Make photos to use as teaching aids throughout the year.

Ask the children to complete the worksheet "Animals of the Bible."

Other Activities

BREAKFAST AND BIBLE STUDY IN THE PARK

RESOURCES
Bibles
bowl
can opener
eggs (1 per person)
hot chocolate or cider
onions (1 per 7 persons)
orange slices
paper products
plastic eating and serving utensils
potatoes (canned/sliced)
sausage (1 lb. per 7 persons)
skillet

PREPARATION
> Purchase food and utensils.

> Chop onions.

PROCEDURE
In a large skillet, cook onions and sausage until brown. Drain. Place in a bowl. Scramble 1 egg per person. Add canned, sliced potatoes. Heat. Add sausage and onion. Heat and stir constantly. Serve with orange slices and hot apple cider or hot chocolate.

Have a Bible study.

TUB SUNDAE

RESOURCES
18-gallon metal tub (new or scrubbed clean)
cherries
chocolate cookies or cereal
ice cream
nuts
plastic spoons
sauces/toppings
whipped topping

PREPARATION
> Purchase food and utensils.

PROCEDURE

Ask the children to put inside the metal tub all the ingredients for an ice cream sundae. Instruct them to mark off their individual "turf" with crumbled chocolate cookies or chocolate cereal.

Distribute plastic spoons for eating.

WESTERN ROUNDUP

RESOURCES

aluminum pie plates and/or frozen dinner plates
bales of hay
cowboy boots
cowboy hats
eating utensils
lassoes
red-checkered tablecloths
saddles
Western attire, decorations, foods, songs

PREPARATION

> Invite "strays" (absentees) from the summer, prospects, children who will promote to your group, and leaders. Ask them to dress in blue jeans, checked shirts, and bandannas.

> Enlist workers and program personalities. Make job assignments.

> Obtain food and decorations.

> Decorate the room with a "corral" and Western items.

> Cover the tables with cloths.

> Set up an area that looks like a chuckwagon.

PROCEDURE

Play Western songs.

Serve Western foods (barbecue and baked beans) in "tin" plates from the chuckwagon.

Present a Western program. Include sing-a-long music with someone playing a guitar.

Notes

[1]Adapted from John and Kaywin LaNoue and Gail Linam, *Promised Land Counselor's Guide for Day Camping* (Nashville: Convention Press, 1983) 59.

[2]Adapted from Fred Wight, *Manners and Customs of Bible Lands* (Chicago: Moody Press, 1953) 294-97.

[3]Marion Armstrong, *Life and Customs in Bible Times* (Nashville: Abingdon Press, 1943) 3.

[4]Adapted from Peter Farb, *The Land, Wildlife, and Peoples of the Bible* (New York: Harper & Row, 1967) 91-92.

[5]Adapted from Wight, 251-57.

[6]Adapted from ibid., 106-107.

[7]Information on goats adapted from ibid., 166-68; and Farb, 43-44.

PLAYING

Participate in

THE WONDERFUL WORLD OF SUMMER OLYMPICS

JUNE 24

12 NN - 2 PM
in the
GREAT HALL

Includes:
Lunch,
Team Selection,
Fun and Games,
competitions to challenge
your every talent!

Bring:
Exercise clothes,
chips, sandwiches, cookies, soft drinks,
Bible

BE READY TO
"GO FOR THE GOLD!!!"

Animals of the Bible

Answer the following questions based on what you learned in class.

(1) How much water can a camel drink at one time?

(2) Why doesn't the hot desert sand hurt the feet of camels?

(3) Identify 3 things sheep were used for.

(4) Identify 2 things goatskin was used for.

(5) Who rode on donkeys?

(6) What were horses mostly used for?

(7) Do lions still live in Israel?

(8) True or False: An eagle eats dead animals; vultures eat live animals.

(9) True or False: Foxes were friends of people.

(10) Are bears ever mentioned in the Bible?

(11) Leopards are members of which animal family?

(12) Who asked his son to bring him deer meat (venison)?

(13) What were quail used for?

(14) When did people eat fatted calves?

Music

Shalom, Chaverim

Sha - lom, cha - ve - rim! Sha - lom, cha - ve - rim! Sha -

lom, sha - lom! Le - hit - ra - ot, le

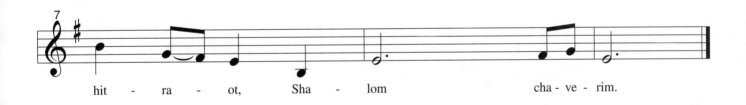

hit - ra - ot, Sha - lom cha - ve - rim.

Palestinian Round. English Words by Bob Jones. From *The Junior Musician*, April-June 1964. © Copyright 1964. The Sunday School Board of the Southern Baptist Convention.

Sing Hosannas

1. Hark to the sto - ry an - gels are tell - ing Of the birth of Je - sus,
2. Shep - herds a - keep - ing watch on the hill - side Heard the won - drous sto - ry,
3. Come, all ye peo - ple, come to the man - ger, Wor - ship and a - dore him;

Born in a man - ger mid cat - tle low - ly Is the Babe most ho - ly.
Knelt down in won - der, gazed at the glo - ry Sud - den - ly ap - pear - ing.
Sing as the an - gels, kneel as the shep - herds, To the Christ our Sav - ior.

Sing, all ye an - gels, Sing, all ye shep - ards! Sing to the lit - tle Babe in the man - ger;

Sing a soft ho - san - na, Sing a loud ho - san - na, Je - sus Christ is born to - day.

Words, Alta C. Faircloth, 1959. Tune MCCRAY, Polish Carol. Arranged, Alta C.Faircloth, 1959. © Copyright 1959, 1964. Renewal 1992, Broadman Press (SESAC). All rights reserved. International copyright secured. Used by permission.

Paul and Silas

1. Paul and Si - las sang in a pris- on, Songs of praise both night and day, An An - gel came and o - pened the gates, Then Paul and Si - las went on their way.

2. Al - ways preach - ing, al- ways prais-ing, Prais - ing God and His wn Son, While oth - ers learned to share their glad - ness, Know - ing Je - sus lov e - 'ry - one.

The God of Abraham Praise

Words, Daniel ben Judah Dayyan, c. 1400. Translated, Newton Mann and Max Landsberg, 1884-85. Alternate tune LEONI. Traditional Hebrew Melody. Transcribed, Meyer Lyon, c. 1770.

Jacob

1. Who was born a twin Man-y years a-go?
2. Who slept on a rock Man-y years a-go?
3. Who kept La-ban's sheep Man-y years a-go?

Who was born a twin; Tell me, do you know?
Who slept on a rock; Tell me, do you know?
Who kept La-ban's sheep; Tell me, do you know?

Chorus

Ja - cob was his name, E - sau was his bro - ther;

I - saac was his dad, Re-bek-ah was his mo - ther;

4. Who had twelve fine sons…
5. Who made peace with God…
6. Who made Joseph's Coat…

Words and melody, Lou Mishler Heath. Arranged, Janelle Taylor.

175

Index

A

Abraham 55, 67
Achan 73
Advent/Christmas 91, 132
Ananias 73
Ark of the Covenant 59, 103, 161
assertiveness 67
aural learners 1, 4

B

Bar Mitzvah 120
barley 15, 16, 93
Bartimaus 18
bathing 108
beards 31
bears 167, 168
Belshazzar 18, 67
Bethany 19, 69, 96
Bethlehem 8, 91, 92, 94
bows and arrows 12, 42, 66
bricks 120
burial customs 19, 20, 97

C

camels 93, 167
camping 159
caravans 87, 93, 167
cattle 168
celebrating 92
chanting 23
chariots 120
children's games 108
city walls and gates 103
clay bowls 12
costume fabrics 18
costumes 29, 31, 33, 77

Creation 134
creative writing 44, 51
cubit 61, 114

D

daily food 107
daily life 106, 108
damaged learners 4, 5
Damascus 114
Daniel 18, 66, 114, 133
dates 40, 80, 82, 88, 108
David 40
Dead Sea 103
deceit 71, 72
deer 166, 168
dependability 65
Desert of Midian 37
donkeys 95, 166, 167
double-reed pipes 145
doves/pigeons 82, 168
dramatic interviews 27
dramatic readings 28

E

Egypt 32, 33, 38, 90, 111
Egyptian fan 12
Engedi 40
Esau 42, 43
Esther 41
eunuch 120

F

fatted calf 57, 168
figs 80, 82, 108, 113, 114
films/filmstrips/videos 117
fishnets 4, 119

Notes

Notes